CIVILIANS IN UNIFORM

CIVILIANS IN UNIFORM
A Memoir: 1937–1945

Richard Terrell

The Radcliffe Press
London · New York

Published in 1998 by
The Radcliffe Press
Victoria House
Bloomsbury Square
London WC1B 4DZ

In the United States of America
and Canada distributed by
St Martin's Press
175 Fifth Avenue
New York
NY 10010

A full CIP record for this book is available from the British Library

A full CIP record for this book is available from the Library of Congress

ISBN 1–86064–236–5

Library of Congress Catalog card number: available

Copy-edited and laser-set by Oxford Publishing Services, Oxford
Printed and bound in Great Britain by WBC Ltd, Bridgend

To Kathleen and George Roche

Contents

Illustrations

1. Advancing along a *chaung* or dried-up stream bed. A party led by a British NCO.
2. A typical scene in country described on our map as 'dense mixed jungle, mainly bamboo'.
3. Making a *basha* with split bamboos.
4. Friendly Khumi tribesmen making bamboo rafts for transporting supplies down the Kaladan river and its tributaries.
5. Khumi tribesmen carrying wounded West Africans to safety.
6. Unarmed carriers bringing supplies from Chiringa.
7. A brown bullock arriving by air from India. Most of the bullocks were white and humped, from the Punjab.

Abbreviations and acronyms

ADC	aide-de-camp
ATS	Auxiliary Territorial Service
CO	Commanding Officer
CB	Companion of the Order of the Bath/ confined to barracks
CBE	Commander of the Order of the British Empire
CP	Central Provinces, *now* Madhya Pradesh
DSO	Companion of the Distinguished Service Order
G1	Chief divisional general staff officer, with rank of Lieutenant-Colonel
GHQ	general headquarters
HQ	headquarters
INA	Indian National Army
KRRC	King's Royal Rifle Corps
LSE	London School of Economics
MC	Military Cross
NAAFI	Navy, Army and Air Force Institutes
NCO	non-commissioned officer
OBE	Officer of the Order of the British Empire
OC	Officer Commanding
P & O	Pacific and Orient shipping line
PEP	Political and Economic Planning
PO	potential officer

Abbreviations and acronyms

PT	physical training
RAF	Royal Air Force
RWAFF	Royal West African Frontier Force
SS	steamship
UP	United Provinces, *now* Uttar Pradesh
WAAF	Women's Auxiliary Air Force

Glossary

basha	hutment (usually made of bamboo)
bucksheesh	a tip or gratuity
bund	handmade earth wall
burka	long enveloping garment worn by Muslim women in public
charpoy	bed made of string and wood
charwallah	tea seller
chaung	dried up stream bed
dhoti	long loincloth worn by men in India
Diwan	chief minister of Maharaja's council
durbar	ceremonial occasion to mark rulership of prince or royal ruler
dushera puja	worship to celebrate end of monsoon
nullah	gully
taung	hill
tiffin	lunch
tonga	horse-drawn trap
vaisya	trader (of the trader caste)

Acknowledgements

A bove all I have to thank my wife Josephine for her encouragement and practical advice on many occasions during the process of putting together the distant memories assembled in these pages. I am especially grateful to Dr Lester Crook, editor of the Radcliffe Press, for his appreciation of my motivation, which has been to retrieve from oblivion personal experiences, many of which were shared with others and valued, if only for that reason.

The Imperial War Museum has permitted me to reproduce the photographs of scenes involving west African troops in the jungles of the Arakan hill tracts of the frontier region of north-western Burma. A copy of this book will be presented to the library of the museum.

In the Postscript I have quoted extensively from *Constitutional Relations between Britain and India: The Transfer of Power*, volume VII (edited by Professor N. Mansergh OBE and Sir Penderel Moon). This is an official document. I am grateful to Mr D. M. Blake, head of the European Manuscripts Section of the British Library, Oriental and India Office Collections, for explaining to me that I am at liberty to reproduce such passages by permission of the Controller of Her Majesty's Stationery Office.

Finally, I am happy to send a copy of this book to Lady Pamela Humphries, surviving daughter of Field Marshall Lord Wavell, who was Viceroy of India throughout my own experience in the region during the war. My reasons for paying tribute to him are explained in the Postscript.

R. T.

August 1997, London

Preface

A close friend with a distinguished war record felt a strong desire to write his war memoirs, assuming that his wife would be good enough to type them out to his dictation. He wished only to leave a written narrative for his grandchildren in the future. His wife put her foot down. 'Men', she declared, 'are obsessed with their war stories, especially on social occasions. I can't stand any of them.' She refused to type out any war memoirs whatever.

Not exactly devoid of such memoirs myself, I said that her stance prompted a distinction between memoirs of wartime and those of war itself. Suppose that I were to produce an account of personal experiences during the Second World War that would include only a few descriptions of military violence but a great deal of other experience only incidentally associated with the war? My narrative would be replete with land and seascapes, magnificent scenery, flights of green parrots over tropical jungle, the calls of baboons from valleys below, colonies of monkeys swinging through the trees, passionate dancing at camps and town halls in Britain and at hill stations in India or dens in Africa, together with many descriptions of individual men and women. How about that? Yes, that would suit her pretty well. The scheme of this book originated in that conversation of about two years ago.

Most of the actual warfare in which I was involved

occurred in a sector of the Burma front that has received little attention from writers and the media generally. The omission is a consequence of the fact that most of the fighting in which British, Indian and American forces took part, occurred hundreds of miles away from the sector familiar to myself, the Arakan hill tracts in the frontier area straddling India and northwestern Burma. Little attention has been given to stories of the two West African divisions in that remote territory. I hope, therefore, that this very personal memoir will contribute a little to general awareness of the Burma scene as a whole.

R. T.
London, 1997

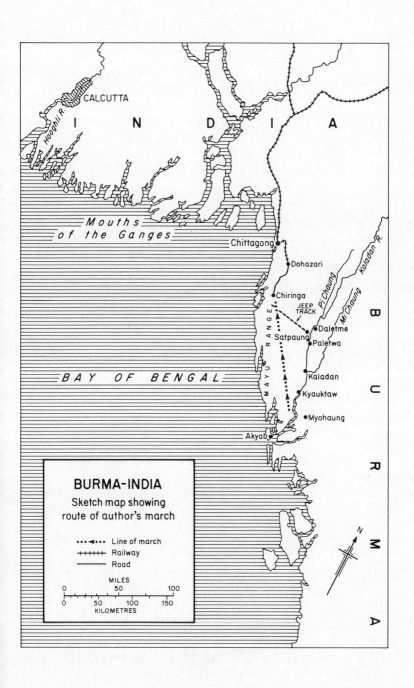

CALCUTTA

Hooghli R.

I   N   D   I   A

Mouths
of the Ganges

Chittagong

Dohazari

Chiringa

JEEP
TRACK

Daletme

P.l Chaung

Mi Chaung

Kaladan R.

B

BAY   OF   BENGAL

MAYU RANGE

Satpaung

Paletwa

Kaladan

Kyauktaw

Myohaung

Akyab

U

R

M

A

N

BURMA-INDIA

Sketch map showing
route of author's march

••••◀•••• Line of march
+++++++ Railway
—————— Road

MILES
0   50   100
0   50   100   150
KILOMETRES

1

At the start

In September 1939 I was 30 years' old, married with two small children and living in a pleasant block of flats in Wandsworth, south London. As a graduate of the London School of Economics, I was a bookish left winger, the author of two books and a lot of book reviews. I earned a small salary as a research secretary on the staff of Political and Economic Planning (PEP), a policy forming organization and luncheon club in Westminster whose members included civil servants, Members of Parliament and miscellaneous intellectuals on the fringes of politics. Talk over lunch every day was often sufficiently voluble as to make me late back in the afternoons at the small corner of the building that I was privileged to call my office. I was thus about as fortunate as any young man could be before the arrival of the national lottery. While it seemed evident from the headlines that the world was about to go up in flames, it did not cross my mind that I might at any time be required to dress up as a soldier and learn about the parts of a Bren gun or an antitank rifle.

My job with PEP preceded my wartime story by about a couple of years. I wish to dwell upon it a little because the experience enabled me to apprehend aspects of war that would otherwise have escaped me.

Most of the club members of PEP formed themselves into groups, each of which applied itself to the study of this or that subject of public interest, such as the organization of

1

the British press, transport or some other aspect of the economy. I became the secretary of a group whose chosen subject was that of industrial relations: that is, the relationships between employers and employees in British economic life. It was called the Partners in Industry group. Such a designation indicated an aspiration to achieve harmonious relationships between two of the three basic requirements of all economic activity: land, labour and capital.

On joining the group as its paid secretary, I very soon realized that the idealism of the group required some kind of schematic plan for their ensuing labours, some system upon which chapter headings might be based. Without any such plan, a printed report would amount to a list of mutually isolated proposals originating in the personal experiences of members of the group. For several weeks I pondered this need for a plan without disclosing my thoughts to anybody else. I felt that the group was floundering in a morass of good intentions.

Eventually, a schematic approach occurred to me. I asked myself how in fact do disputes in industry arise? I was not thinking of enormous strikes or lockouts, but the unreported daily frictions of the ordinary workplace. The answer seemed to depend mainly on the nature of the industry concerned. In the building industry, for example, the construction of a large building involves the grouping of various kinds of workers — steel men, rivetters, concrete mixers, bricklayers, tilers, carpenters, joiners, plasterers, painters and many others. Such grouping is intended to last only for a specified period and for particular phases of the job. Throughout the period of construction, each group of workers, with its own trade union leadership, will struggle to get the best possible deal for its members, and the scope for friction is limitless. In such an industry, the key figures will be those responsible for making decisions about the short-term groupings of workers required from the beginning until the end of the entire job. Over-aggressive bargaining will damage the interests of capital. Weakness on the part of the principal entrepreneur will encourage labour to damage its own interests. In such an industry, the key figures are the foremen on one side and the trade union shop stewards on the other. The emotive word 'partners' implies some kind of short-term equilibrium between otherwise conflicting interests. In Ibsen's play *The Master Builder*, the 'Master' is a stage character of the author's imagination. In the real world of Britain in 1937, he could occupy the biggest desk in London or, beneath a steel helmet and a yellow plastic cape, order men about on the site.

A very different state of affairs will prevail in another kind of industry, say the manufacture of cigarettes on a big scale, the production of large numbers of identical objects of any kind: such as a particular model of a motorcar, uniforms for policemen or postmen or soldiers, electric kettles, ball-point pens or paper clips, or perhaps zip fasteners. Here the image of a conveyor belt comes to mind with Charlie Chaplin going off his head with a couple of large spanners or, best of all, the scenes of the gramophone factory in René Clair's famous film *A Nous la Liberté*. Some will remember the theme melody:

> *Si vous désirez un emploi*
> *Ecrivez votre nom avec le main droit.*
> *Apres avoir fait cela, tournez à gauche*
> *Et marche tout droit!*
> *Le travail: c'est obligatoire!*
> *Le travail: c'est la liberté!*

In all such industries, harmonious industrial relationships depend upon the establishment of psychologically endurable routines of work for everybody in the factory. This depends on human relationships and the intuitive skills of personnel management. Workers must not merely be paid but must feel that their repetitive work is appreciated by the firm, or valued for some other reason (especially in wartime). The bad manager is identified by personal traits. If approached by a worker who wants half a day off to visit her dying mother, he will allow the worker to stand silently before his desk, waiting for him to mutter 'Yes?' without looking up from a paper, instead of smiling and saying: 'Yes, Jenny, can I help you?'

Such thoughts led me to set out a general plan of research for the Partners in Industry group. Our chairman was Lawrence Neal (later Sir Lawrence Neal) head of Daniel Neal, the famous store for children's wear in London. I suggested to him that we should select a modest group of industries, each more or less typical of my two main types: constructional, 'job' or conveyor belt industries, or 'routine' industries. I, as the secretary, would travel about the country visiting the sites of all our selected industries, arrange meetings with key personalities concerned with each kind, and draft chapters for the group to consider in London. Each chapter would conclude with a list of policy recommendations appropriate to the industry described. After much argument, in two or three meetings my plan was approved. I learnt more about the world of work during the ensuing two years than ever before or since.

The reader will ask: what has all this to do with the rest of this book? The armed forces on both sides in the Second World War made heavy demands on engineering industries, but such industries were not all of the same kinds during the prewar years. Those of Germany, Italy and Japan were dominated largely by 'routine' rather than constructional or 'job'-like technology. It was this characteristic that enabled them, in the middle and late 1930s, very rapidly to expand their production of identical products, including military aircraft, tanks, armoured vehicles, munitions of many kinds and submarines. All this explains the phenomenon known as the blitzkrieg.

The engineering industries of Britain over many decades from the mid-nineteenth century to the 1930s, were different. They were largely of a constructional or 'job'-like structure, involving many kinds of civil engineering. The industrial revolution itself was an outstanding achievement in these fields. British companies undertook highly specialized tasks on behalf of governments and private enterprise overseas. Examples are the construction of a large proportion of the railways of North and South America, tramways, gasworks, bridges, pumps for irrigation schemes, power generating projects, and waterworks of many kinds. Each of such projects was, as it were, tailor-made for the investor in Britain or overseas. In short, ours was not a 'blitzkrieg' economy, and it was basically for this reason that it took no less than four years (from Dunkirk in 1940 to the Normandy landings in the summer of 1944) and vast assistance from the United States, to equip the British armed forces for their part in the ultimate defeat of the Axis powers both in the West and the East.

That experience contributed also to a close personal interest in the former occupations of the men who surrounded me in the army. Ever since the Napoleonic wars the British had been called a nation of shopkeepers. In the Second World War, the British armed forces could more accurately be described as an army of shop assistants. In the First World War, our armed forces were not exclusively assembled from the mass of workers not needed for the making of munitions. In that war, munitions were largely produced by women, thus releasing men for war service. In the Second World War, recruitment was more elaborate, partly by means of the 'Schedule of Reserved Occupations', and partly by the development of the system of employment exchanges. People in possession of knowledge or skills essential for war industries were not called up for military service. The employment exchanges enabled employers in war industries to recruit labour much more efficiently than had ever been possible before.

* * *

The London blitz in the summer of 1940 made it impossible for our Partners in Industry group to continue its work. Many of the members had left London altogether to escape the blitz so that meetings became impossible. Paper rationing made publication impracticable and the introduction of governmental regulations of manpower made most of our work out of date anyway. I found myself redundant, waiting to be called up with my age group, but still allowed to receive my salary from PEP. The situation was demoralizing: so much so that I asked to be dismissed, with the intention of getting into the army as soon as possible.

My employers agreed to 'let me go', but before dismissing me they allowed me to produce a special broadsheet on the working of employment exchanges.

One of the members of the group was T. S. Chegwidden (later Sir Thomas Chegwidden), then an assistant secretary at the Ministry of Labour and National Service. He introduced me to colleagues in the ministry who, in turn, enabled me to visit important exchanges up and down the country. My report, only a few pages in length, made recommendations, which, I like to think, contributed a little to the postwar establishment of the modern system of job centres. I remember suggesting, also, that every town should have a social services centre at which members of the public would be able to seek information about the wide range of new services then looming upon the horizon of the future with the welfare state as envisaged by Sir William Beveridge (as he then was). The subsequent development of the Citizens' Advice Bureaux and legal aid were germinating in the minds of colleagues long ago.

2
Bombed out

On the night of the first day of the war, 3 September 1939, I was alone in the flat, the children having been evacuated to Cornwall and Dorset, and my wife was visiting friends in Sussex. The night was warm and I lay on the bed loosely covered by a white sheet, my gas mask at the ready on a bedside table. Air raid precautions were a sensible business but I had not paid sufficient attention to them to distinguish between the various signals of wardens in the streets. I lay wondering whether the presence of gas was to be indicated by the blowing of a whistle or the twirl of a rattle. Anyway, in a little while I heard the moaning of an air raid siren and the distant drone of a single aircraft, coming from a great altitude. Then followed one of the wardens' noises, whether a whistle or a rattle, or perhaps both, I do not recall. To be on the safe side, I carefully donned the gas mask and waited for the end of the world, whose only symptoms would probably take the form of some kind of suddenness.

Hearing a faint knocking on the front door, I wrapped the sheet closely round my body and went to open it. In the doorway stood two old ladies from another flat. Confronted by the spectre which I presented to them in my horrible, snout-like mask and ghostly attire, they stumbled, aghast, against the wall, unable to utter a word. I had just enough presence of mind to grasp that they were not dying of gas poisoning, but merely of fright. I removed the mask, smiled

9

and invited them to come in. They at once recovered and one of them said: 'Oh Mr Terrell, may we sit with you till we are all killed together?' 'Certainly,' I replied. 'I'll just make a pot of tea.'

They sat together on the sofa while I administered the tea. I tried to persuade them that a single aircraft circling many thousands of feet above the millions of human beings in London would not be likely to kill our particular selves rather than any other no less deserving characters hidden in the blackout below. Such arguments were in vain. My guests were convinced that we should never again see the light of day. I told them that, whatever might happen during the rest of the night, I must get some sleep before going to work the next morning. They were welcome to continue to sit on the sofa, come what may. In the morning they had gone.

* * *

The enormity of war for us in Britain did not manifest itself until the spring of the following year with the fall of France, the withdrawal from Dunkirk, the replacement of Chamberlain by Churchill and the blitzkrieg of the Luftwaffe, intended to herald the invasion of the country. Perhaps the most momentous event of that time was the raid on the old wooden docks of London in daylight on 7 September 1940. From the windows of the flat we could see the flames, smell the dense black smoke and watch the dogfights overhead. The most awful spectacle was an aircraft spiralling down to crash below, beyond distant buildings, unseen, unidentified in the sunshine of death.

On that same day our own block of flats was straddled by bombs, which hit and destroyed several buildings in the same street. As we heard the bombs whistling down upon us, we instinctively flung ourselves face down on the beds, shielding our heads with our arms. I remember the feeling that the whole building was swaying, and glancing towards a window beyond which a vast cloud of dust was rising, causing us to choke. Our faces and hair were smothered in the dust of crashing brickwork. Through the rising dust, on the other side of the street, could be seen the remains of a large, tall private house. Its entire side wall had collapsed, revealing the interiors of rooms on four storeys — beds, chairs, tables, carpets, resembling the contents of a doll's house. Far up, a lavatory pan hung upon a length of piping. Water streamed from a tube.

In a short lull we heard the voices of wardens in the gardens below our block: 'You've got three minutes to get out. Time bombs in the gardens.' They shouted the words again and again. My mother-in-law had come to lunch with us that day: indeed she had cooked for us a leg of lamb in our oven. She left at once to return to her home in another part of south London.

A personal friend, whose home was in Hampstead, close to the Heath, was staying elsewhere, in Essex. Before going away with his wife and children he had told me (and other friends in London) that if any of us were 'bombed out' we could make use of his Hampstead home. At once we grabbed a few sheets and blankets — I took a book from a shelf — my wife carried the hot joint on a dish. We walked down the street with other refugees to the nearest underground station (itself crowded with people preparing to spend the night on its platforms), travelled to Belsize Park in Hampstead, and walked from there to my friend's house.

There we found every room full of refugees, many homeless, some with nothing but the clothes on their bodies. My wife and I found a small space on the concrete floor of a basement room.

During the next few weeks the community of refugees worked out a scheme for living. With the aid of small sums of money in the form of 'war damage compensation' from the local employment exchange, they agreed that each woman would undertake the catering for the rest on a daily rota basis. And so we survived.

After about three days, I returned to our flat in Wandsworth to collect a few belongings. There I found a caretaker who described how the flats had all been burgled by a bogus furniture removal outfit. The flats had been stripped of all their relatively portable contents.

In his quarters at the back of the block he showed me twenty or thirty women's handbags and men's wallets and briefcases spread along benches. No money had been left in any of them. All the remaining items of furniture in the flats were about to be stored in a warehouse by the local authority, and would be available for collection by the owners at their convenience.

I was, perhaps understandably, too preoccupied with the loss of our own family belongings to give any thought to the two old ladies whom I had so scared a year before. It is perhaps no accident that, after the war, during my service in Whitehall, I spent several years in a schedule of work concerned with the treatment of offenders against the criminal law. Nobody has yet discovered very much about the workings of the criminal mind, including those that culminated in the theft of our belongings between air raids.

On my return to Hampstead, I wrote to the Ministry of Labour and National Service and requested to be called up into the army as soon as possible. My Westminster job had been made impossible by the air raids and I did not want to be unemployed at such a time. There was too much broken glass in the streets for a spell of idleness to retain much of its charm.

Bombed out

On 17 October 1940, I became a recruit at a training centre of the King's Royal Rifle Corps at Bushfield barracks, near Winchester. My military guise was assumed on that day and continued until mid-December 1945, when a troopship arrived at Southampton on a foggy morning.

3

Civilians in uniform

The heading of this chapter gives meaning to the word 'guise', which hovers over all my war years and those of most of my contemporaries of both sexes. The same word serves to indicate the transformations of the lives of civilians by the realities of war, for example, the building manager who becomes a blackout expert, the manageress of a country club who is put in charge of clothing coupons in a government office, and the soft furnisher who now manufactures army socks.

My wife, some time in 1940, while still a housewife with two children, quickly assumed another guise. Possessing good academic qualifications and shrewd intelligence, she became one of about forty women who, after a course of training, academic and industrial, became labour managers in the wartime engineering industries in Britain. Throughout the war and for a few years afterwards, she held such a position in an important electrical engineering factory in west London. Her war was a very urban affair of bombs, machinery, tea breaks, trade unions and gritty arguments interrupted by the moans of sirens. Mine was different, a sequence in rural technicolour, mostly green and brown, with a smell of tropical wood smoke.

The King's Royal Rifle Corps (KRRC), in which I became a rifleman, was a London regiment, in the sense that most of the men were Londoners. That was not true of the officers, for most of them seemed to belong to the squirearchy and some had rather grand rural backgrounds. Having a university degree I was at first classified as a 'PO' or potential officer who could expect to be sent away to an officer cadet training unit within a few weeks. That did not occur, however, for security reasons. My book about the Soviet Union, published in 1937, had marked me down as a communist, and it is true that I had been a member of the party from that date until the outset of the war when I became disillusioned by its policies. For a long time under a cloud, therefore, I spent the first half of my military life as a rifleman and the rest as an officer.

* * *

Within a few days of my new life in the guise of a soldier it surprised me to observe that the overwhelming majority of the men by whom I was surrounded for so long affected a cynical attitude to the very existence of the army in which they served and to any notions about 'war aims', however defined. Affectation, however, implies pretence, whether conscious or not. I suspect that such pretence had a sexual root. Deprived of their womenfolk for long stretches of time, soldiers gave vent to their frustration in loud voices laced with humour, often very funny indeed. Officers and NCOs fully appreciated this and expressed their understanding with a responsive humour of their own.

The language of all concerned was not considered suitable in the company of women of any kind. Nobody knows what the women felt about it. Anyway, extreme outspokenness was not confined to sex, but extended to every other topic from defecation to politics. I remember an amiable man who, in a gloomy, stone-cold barrack room in Norfolk, said loudly: 'F**k! I've a good mind to get an interview with the

CO. I'll tell him I've become a conscientious objector on political grounds. We'd be better off under the f**kin' Germans.' A few others muttered 'Hear! Hear!' We were very demoralized at that stage. Not many of us considered that the Germans, struggling in the Russian snow, were probably in no mind to invade East Anglia just then. They, and we too, were listening to other songs.

At virtually all the camps and barracks where troops were stationed, canteens where established by the NAAFI (Navy, Army and Air Force Institutes) organization. Apart from miscellaneous confectionery, snacks, hair oil, toothpaste and beer at times, there was usually a piano in need of tuning and at least a couple of soldiers able to strum in their overcoats, while lines of men queued with their mugs before big cans of purplish tea during mid-morning breaks.

What were the songs that moved us then? Hardly any of them were of a martial nature, whatever the state of the world at the time. Virtually all expressed ineffable yearning for love everlasting. I remember a small, strongly built man from the Whitechapel Road whose name was Jack Kemp. In peacetime he had been an undertaker-cum-florist and the business was still being run by his relatives. Sitting at the piano he sang every day with great vigour a song of considerable length that went more or less like this:

> *Don't ever pass me by!*
> *Just say Hello to an old flame!*
> *Our love will never die!*
> *I keep rememberin' your name!*
> *All that's between us. ...*
> *Somebody lied. ...*
> *It's just foolish pride!*
> *Oh let us name the day, dear,*
> *Don't ever pass me by.*

17

Jack's voice was extremely powerful and he could have gripped a whole cinema full of people. Whenever he returned from short spells of leave he brought with him a huge bunch of flowers to stand on the barrack-room table, and would sing his song with passion without pausing to remove his overcoat. We would follow him anywhere, a natural leader of men.

There were many other songs snatches I remember, most of them emanating from a small scratchy radio up on the ceiling of our Nissen hut.

> *Amapola! My pretty little Poppy,*
> *How long would it take me*
> *To be near if you beckoned?*
> *Less than a second,*
> *Less than a second!*
> *Only for ever! If you care to know!*
> *Yours till the end of life's story!*
> *For I was born to be just Yours.*

Whenever the voice of Vera Lynn could be heard from the box on the ceiling, men flung themselves down on the beds and closed their eyes.

My introduction to the humorous obscenities of soldiers' speech came during the first days of strenuous drill at the Nissen-hutted camp at Bushfield barracks near Winchester. Our sergeant was a small, twinkling regular soldier in his middle forties who had served most of his time on the North-West Frontier of India, a region replete with anec- dotes of farcical obscenity. He would shout at us at the top of his voice:

> Squaaad. Atten-TION!
> Stand at EASE!

Stand at EASE I said!
Feet 18 inches apart!
Don't be afraid!
Nothink won't drop aht!

As we marched about the gravelly square performing elaborate, ballet-like drills with our rifles, he would yell:

Swing them f**kin' arms!
Rifleman George X your limbs is all stiff!
Get a proper woman tonight and get yerself
relaxed for f**k's sake!
Left right, left right, left right.
That's better!
I'll make soldiers of you mob.
Wait and see!

Within a couple of weeks certain men with personal problems wanted to confide in me and sometimes seek my assistance. This experience gave me the feeling that I was becoming a welfare officer of sorts. Here are three cases that I remember especially. In our barrack room we were all supposed to be 31 years' old. One of us, however, was obviously older. He told me, in whispers, that he was actually 41 and had been called up by mistake instead of his brother who was exactly ten years younger. This created two problems for him. First, he found some of the training too strenuous and feared lest he might collapse with a heart attack. Second, if he were to tell his story to an officer he might be discharged. Since his peacetime job had disappeared long ago he would be unemployed as a civilian. 'So I'm in a bit of a jam, see.' I asked him if there was not some job in the company office that he could do without risk to his heart. I do not remember whether or not I took any action, but within a few days of our conversation he was given a stripe and a job looking after stocks of clothing in the quartermaster's store. As a former clerk he could not have done better.

Another man told me he had received a letter from a neighbour near his civilian home who said that the man's wife was having an affair with a 'f**kin' RAF man'. It was obviously necessary that he should apply for compassionate leave in order to 'do her in'.

I said: 'Do you mean that you want compassionate leave to commit a murder?' His reply was: 'Bugger murder. I'll kill the bitch.'

'What about the RAF man. Will you kill him too?'

'I dunno. Maybe.'

I asked for time to consider the situation. Eventually, over a pint of beer in the NAAFI, I said something like this: 'You have been married to your wife for several years and she is the mother of your kids. Now think. Can you really imagine life without that woman? And besides, what kind of an affair is she supposed to be having with the RAF man? We all want sex in this dump. What about her? Think.' I do not believe that any murders were committed.

One of our number was a cadaverous looking Irishman with a strange scar on his left cheek and somewhat incoherent speech. I do not remember his real name, but he was generally known as Nelson or Death Warmed Up. In a long session he told me his story. He had been born in a village somewhere to the west of Dublin. His father was a brute who hated the child.

One day, in a fury, his father had thrust a hot poker into his son's cheek and injured his tongue, which permanently affected his speech. He then became determined to get away from his father. On the docks in Dublin, he managed to smuggle himself into a ship transporting live cattle to Liverpool by hiding beneath the legs of a cow. From Liverpool, he had walked and begged his way to London where he had met an Irish woman from his own village and they had settled down together.

Nelson had never learned to read or write, but he had somehow managed to keep this completely secret in the army. He wanted my help in two ways. Would I write an occasional letter to his woman friend at his dictation, and read to him any replies from her. I asked him how he managed to find out what his duties were to be if he could not read the 'detail board' every morning. His solution to that problem was ingenious.

As soon as the detail board was put up on a wall, Nelson would wait till about twenty men had gathered in front of it. Only then would he go to the back of the crowd. After a few seconds, he would ask any man who happened to be standing near the board to let him know if Nelson would be on 'spud peeling', 'company office cleaning', 'on guard duty' or 'cookhouse fatigue' that day. This dodge always seemed to work well enough, but Nelson would be grateful if I would glance at the detail board each day just to make sure that he had got it right.

In subsequent weeks, dealing with Nelson's correspondence, I discovered what a shrewd, intelligent man he really was. He was clever in dealing with the moans of his wife, wisely deciding when to be soothing or when to say nothing in reply to her questions.

My long spell as a rifleman was spent in 'dumps' in various parts of southern England, the mountains of Wales, East Anglia and the New Forest in Hampshire. All such stations were situated in beautiful countryside within walking distance of small towns or villages. At those in western parts of the country, men were undergoing technical training of many kinds.

Every recruit was required to become a specialist of one kind or another. I received several weeks of training as a signaller. Other men became gunners, motor drivers, motor mechanics and various kinds of engineers and experts in the subject of land mines or chemical warfare or catering.

Armies are vast schools and colleges, imparting skills that are never wholly lost to their possessors. During my spell in the New Forest it was intended that I should be trained as a sergeant instructor in the strange new subject called 'battle drill', which I greatly enjoyed because it seemed like some kind of bizarre ballet.

I did not, however, complete that training because I was suddenly whisked away to the Isle of Man as a cadet for training as an infantry officer. At all the stations in East Anglia the motorized infantry battalion to which I belonged formed part of the only fully equipped armoured division in Britain.

In this short book, I shall not attempt to describe all the various 'dumps' at which I was stationed. Instead, I shall settle for a few brief anecdotes and vignettes, to convey an impression of a largely forgotten epoch.

During our long spell at Chiseldon barracks beneath the Marlborough Downs, I became a member of a special 'demonstration platoon' whose job was to perform manœuvres as visual aids to bodies of other troops. Standing on high ground they could watch our performances under instructions of their own officers. Such training is unavoidably schematic and abstract, for most real warfare becomes for its participants a seeming chaos of noise and confusion.

Our platoon commander was an aristocratic young man whom we all respected and admired. As a sort of treat he arranged for us to spend a week on our own under canvas in a farming area high on the Downs in the middle of June. We occupied several tents arranged to accommodate our miniature force, with its own commissariat and arms (Bren guns), signals and operational staff.

During one night I was on sentry duty close to the signals tent with its wireless set for receiving and sending messages to other units spread over the region. I shall never forget the experience of standing motionless before dawn in that beautiful rural atmosphere of dew-laden mist in which little could be discerned but the outlines of the hills against the sky and the form of an ancient tree.

Occasionally, I could hear the twitter of a bird, but from the tent behind me came an endless stream of radio signals, forming, as it were, a panorama of sound throughout the night. Each sound expressed a human purpose. Together, they formed a collective mystery. They resembled, too, the myriad lights of a city seen from a hilltop or an aircraft, each point of light the source of human purpose, yet forming a whole whose meaning is beyond all quest. As the dawn broke a darkness in my immediate foreground became a cow whose ears began to twitch.

* * *

It was not long before I acquired a reputation as a cook. This went back to my childhood, for my mother, until her marriage had for several years been an instructress at the National School of Cookery in the Buckingham Palace Road, London. She always provided delicious food for the family, either herself or by supervising a servant. The kitchen was always the most important part of any of our dwellings.

In military camps in various parts of the country, men sat for meals in groups of twelve, three on each side of a square table. One day I got myself into trouble. I and a few others decided that the meat in the stew tasted and smelt rancid.

23

When the orderly officer of the day reached our table, we all stood up — the usual form of salute on such occasions. The orderly sergeant said roughly: 'Any complaints?'

'Yes, Sir', I said. 'Some of us feel that the meat is a bit off.' The officer glanced round the table and asked if anyone else agreed with my statement. Nobody uttered a word.

Later that day a messenger arrived at our barrack room and said: 'Is Rifleman Terrell here?'

'That's me,' I replied.

'You're on a charge for making a frivolous complaint.'

As soon as the messenger had gone there was silence. Then one of the men said loudly: 'Bloody shame! Joe (my nickname) was dead right. The meat stank. I'll be a witness and support Joe.'

A few days later I was summoned to appear before our company commander, an elderly, rubicund regular officer who had returned from retirement to help his old regiment during the war. When conducting trials of men on minor disciplinary charges he brought with him a large pet sheep dog named George, which sat beside the desk. Every now and then he would turn to the dog and say: 'Well, George, what do you say to that?' or say sagely: 'George agrees entirely.' Anybody who tittered at the joke of George would be sternly rebuked by the company sergeant major.

Such trials were conducted with a terrifying ritual, the details of which I have largely forgotten. Men required to appear for trial had to stand in a line outside the company office, often shivering in bitterly cold weather. The door would open and a voice from within would call: 'Rifleman X,' in my case 'Rifleman Terrell.' A sergeant shouted 'cap off!' I removed my cap. 'Quick march! Left right, left right, left right halt!'

As I stood there at attention the old officer said: 'What's the charge?' The sergeant rattled off the story of how I had described the stew as rancid and how none of the other men at the table had agreed with me.

Then the officer said: 'What are all those men standing outside for?' The sergeant replied: 'They're all witnesses in support of Rifleman Terrell, Sir!' 'Well, sergeant, get them all into the office and we'll see what they have to say.' About ten men were marched in and stood in a line at attention. The officer said: 'Rifleman Terrell, what have you to say?' I described the story, ending with 'Sir!'

The sergeant had a list of the names of the witnesses, which he handed to the officer. Each man was asked to give his evidence and all, except one, said simply: 'I agree with Rifleman Terrell, Sir!' The exceptional witness was a Polish Jew from the Commercial Road in east London whose name was something like 'Rifleman Izvolsky'. When asked to give his evidence he said: 'I thought the meat was tasteless, Sir!'

'Tasteless, you say. That's the first time I have heard of bad meat being tasteless. Strange, eh George? The dog nodded. The sergeant said: 'He means "distasteful" Sir!'

'Well well,' said the officer: 'Case dismissed.'

Everybody marched out immediately and the next case was called. When we got back to the barrack room I thanked the men for their wonderful support, and they expressed their approval of the old man and his dog.

Had I been found guilty my punishment would perhaps have been 'seven days CB', or 'confined to barracks'. Such punishment was known as 'jankers'. Confinement to barracks would have prevented me from leaving the camp for any purpose, no visits to the cinema, no cups of tea in cafés, no dances, no meetings with girlfriends, no walks in the country. Instead, I would be kept busy peeling potatoes, scrubbing out the floor of the barrack room with very dirty water and doing extra guard duties. Instead, I could listen to Vera Lynn and go to dances as much as I liked.

As for cooking, whenever we went on manœuvres, each little group of a few men was responsible for cooking its own food, either by using a portable spirit stove or by making fires with bits of wood picked up from hedgerows. We carried raw meat and vegetables in the vehicles. We were an entirely motorized unit and my job was that of a Bren gunner in a section of three Bren carriers. These were light armoured open decked tracked vehicles. The crew of each carrier included three men, the driver, an assistant and the Bren gunner. A section, therefore included nine men. Each vehicle carried spare fuel, tools, blankets, a stove and rations, with a 'dixie' or kettle. Each man carried his own mess tin, mug and cutlery. It was inadvisable to lose any of this gear. I became the cook for our section.

Whenever I went to London on leave I would visit Soho and buy such things as cloves of garlic, chillies, curry powder, cumin, bay leaf and rock salt, all of which I carried in a small biscuit tin tucked into my kitbag.

One day, in a field I found a broken gridiron upon which I could set the dixie for making a stew, and I always took with me a very sharp knife for trimming meat and preparing vegetables. I would cut meat into small cubes, beat them hard and produce stews that all the men in the section enjoyed. I never told them about my use of garlic, spices and gravy powder, because the mention of such things would have seemed horrific to them. Nobody could explain the smells from our section, which drifted agreeably over landscapes in East Anglia, the Marlborough Downs and the glorious hills of mid-Wales.

Every evening, at about 6.30 or 7.00, a bugle call from the cookhouse announced that an optional supper was available. Usually hungry, I would grab my 'eating irons' and go over to the cookhouse canteen to enjoy whatever was going. One evening, on my return to the barrack room after such a meal, one or two of the men asked me: 'What's for supper, Joe?' 'Fish', I replied. 'Oh! F**kin' fish.' They turned away their faces in disgust. A few moments later another man went to the canteen for supper. On his return he said: 'Smashin' supper tonight. Fish 'n chips!' Everybody sat up. 'Fish 'n chips' Joe said it was *fish*, f**kin' fish!' There was a general rush to the canteen in the hope of eating some of the precious viand before the supply was exhausted.

A similar conservatism was expressed in matters of clothing. Troops would not think of removing a warm pullover in hot sunshine, but would continue to sweat in discomfort. And, in cold weather, they would not bother to put on a pullover, but would shiver accordingly.

In one matter, British soldiers were obliged to behave in a manner quite at variance with their natural selves. As British human beings, they are skilled distributors of litter, able to scatter it evenly over every beauty spot, urban park or coastal beach within reach. In the army, their yearnings for litter were frustrated, no scrap of it being allowed to adorn any spot at which anything edible or drinkable had been consumed. The suffering caused by such deprivation is beyond calculation.

I remember standing in a long queue waiting for a mug of tea during a morning break. At the time Japanese forces had just overrun Burma and seemed about to conquer Assam with its tea gardens. I said to one of my companions in the queue something like: 'Maybe we'll get no tea at all if the Japs get Assam.' The response was revealing. 'Cor. An Englishman's got a *right* to a cup o' tea, ain't 'e?' 'No,' I replied. 'Nobody has a right to any tea at all, but we may have to fight for it some day.'

* * *

While no part of Britain was entirely spared the danger of attack from the air, most of the bombs fell on urban areas and very few army camp sites were hit. This had interesting implications for national morale, and presumably affected other countries as well as Britain. Soldiers visiting their urban homes on leave felt that their wives, girlfriends and neighbours were the real victims of the war, while they themselves lived in comparative safety. Women and neighbours, however, felt that their husbands and boyfriends were being preserved, as it were, for death on the battlefields of the Middle East, the Far East, North Africa and, some day, Europe itself.

The initiating period of training for recruits at Bushfield barracks was seven weeks. One evening within the first few days of my own 'intake', the camp was bombed; a Nissen-hutted barrack room was completely destroyed, and several recruits were killed and more wounded.

Each day we looked forward to a moment in the late afternoon when we were allowed to walk down the hill to Winchester in 'walking out dress' (elaborately cleaned and pressed battledress) but always carrying gas masks, steel helmets and rifles (unloaded), presumably to remind us of our military identity outside the camp. Our destinations included the cinema, dance halls, cafés, pubs, reading rooms and libraries, in which letters were written.

The air-raid sirens sounded while I was walking up the wooded roadway to the camp. Just as I reached the sentry box and the wide gate, I heard the sudden noise of an aircraft swooping down and the whistle of falling bombs, sounds almost identical to those recalled from the bombing of our Wandsworth flat.

At once I flung myself down on the concrete roadway and felt the inadequacy of my helmet for the protection of my back and limbs against shrapnel or machine-gun fire. As the bombs crashed a few yards away, I felt the earth heaving and glimpsed the rising dust. Within a few seconds, the plane was gone and a terrible silence ensued. In a shaky voice the sentry let me through and I walked to my own barrack room, which had not been hit. Dead bodies were removed silently during the night and the wounded taken to hospitals in Winchester. In the morning I saw what appeared to be lumps of flesh smothered in grey dust. Our senses never reveal to us the whole of any event. We become aware only of more or less.

I cannot say, for I do not know, how the bombing affected our morale as recruits. During war it appears to its participants that only power can be affected by loss or gain. Morale, more elusive, remains for leadership to sustain.

* * *

As mentioned earlier, in 1942 I was sent away on a course of training in 'battle drill' at a commandeered country house in the New Forest in Hampshire. Since I was debarred from becoming an officer because of my politics, it was hoped that after the special training I could become a sergeant-instructor in battle drill. It was thought that I had a commanding parade ground voice, and I certainly enjoyed my experience with the other trainees, who came from units all over the country. We were not allowed to walk for any purpose at all (even to go to the loo) and ran everywhere, always carrying a rifle. While the drills seemed more like rehearsals for a ballet than for any real warfare, they did involve an abstract logic that was convincing. The experience caused me to ponder over the value of any kind of drill in military training. One difficulty is that nobody can think of anything else anyway.

One day, however, I was sent for by an officer from the War Office who told me that, after all, it had been decided that I ought to become an officer and that, within a few weeks I should be sent to an officer cadet training unit. In the meantime, I would be made a lance corporal and sent back to my battalion, then stationed somewhere near the Marlborough Downs. The officer said with a smile: 'If you are to command a platoon of 30 men, you might as well show that you can command a section of nine men.'

A little later, a friend told me gravely that the sudden change in my destiny must be attributed to a bomb that had caused the evanescence of the secret file about my past as a dangerous communist. However fanciful that explanation might seem, my subsequent story does not seem incompatible with the bomb theory.

As soon as I became a lance corporal my nickname was dropped and I was thereafter addressed as 'Corp'. Within a few days, too, I was told that I had been elected (or perhaps appointed) as secretary of the corporals' club. In the army, men did not bother much about the 'how' of decisions, but accepted them as facts, however disagreeable, dotty or irksome they might seem. My responsibilities, however, seemed quite onerous. Smartly dressed I was expected to keep order in the corporals' part of the NAAFI, see that all litter was removed before closing time and that all the chairs and tables were tidily arranged for the following day. I very soon learned the folly of being too bossy with British soldiers.

One of my jobs was to round up women for dances at the club. This involved visiting nearby camps for women, such as the WAAF (Women's Auxiliary Air Force), the ATS (Auxiliary Territorial Service) and the women's Land Army. I had to arrange for lorries to collect groups of women from these camps, ensure that they were all safely returned to their camps before midnight, and provide them with blankets to prevent them from catching cold. All this involved discussions with the various women's commandants, some of whom were most fearsome ladies.

One occasion involving women is especially memorable. In motorized units such as ours, it was customary for the driver of a vehicle to arrange for it to break down in a village containing a good café where repasts of 'egg on chips', 'apple pie' or even 'bacon and eggs' were available. Such meals, whatever their real ingredients, were all known as 'egg and slice'.

Anywhere in, say Swindon or Thetford could be heard snatches of conversation among soldiers: 'We was just 'avin egg and slice when this tart come in and asks if any of us was good for a quid.' Or: 'We was doin' nothink but 'avin egg and slice when a f**kin' red cap sergeant (police) comes in and tells us to get back to camp, the bastard.'

The driver of my Bren carrier contrived to break down one sunny afternoon at a café in a hamlet near a plantation of conifers belonging to the Forestry Commission. About a hundred yards from the café I noticed a small group of young Land Army women who were evidently working for the Commission. I walked over to them and spoke to a tall blonde with bright blue eyes, yellow hair and skin tanned by the sun:

'Good afternoon. I'm the secretary of the corporals' club at the KRRC camp at X. We're having a dance next Wednesday and I wonder if any of you would like to come along.' The young woman said: 'What sort of men have you got?' I said: 'Londoners, mostly.'

'Londoners! Oh, maybe we could come, but you will have to fix it with the commandant. She's at that house over there.' I knocked at the door. It was opened by a ladylike woman in civilian dress. She was prepared for 'her girls' to come to our dance, but, she said: 'I must have them all back here in the village by midnight, and I don't want any of them to catch cold.' I made my usual promises and added that I would provide hot tea for them as well as blankets.

At the dance itself, the Land Army women, unlike the others, did not wear their daytime uniforms, which were most repugnant as ballroom attire. All appeared in evening dress with earrings, bangles, necklaces and lovely combs in their hair. This created a problem, for the men craved to dance with them to the neglect of the women in uniforms, however embraceable the latter might seem to the discerning among us.

During the winter months of 1941/2, Britain's military prospects were pretty grim. So far as we were concerned, the grimness made itself felt by the austerity of our training. This took two forms. First, there were the long marches without our vehicles. This entailed marching all day on nothing but a crust of bread and a little water, sleeping out on wet, cold ground with insufficient covering, scrambling through barbed wire and getting across rivers by using ropes suspended above the water, making all movements 'at the double', and a great deal of realistic 'field firing' (the use of live ammunition of various kinds) in imaginary uphill attacks on strongly held and imaginary enemy positions. Life became very strenuous indeed.

Second, our battalion of motorized infantry formed a small part of the Sixth Armoured Division, which, after decades of peacetime 'disarmament', was now the only completely equipped armoured division in Britain. We were deployed over vast stretches of East Anglia and intended to defend the region against possible invasion from across the North Sea. The task implied that the divisional staff had to be trained in the movements of thousands of troops of all arms (infantry, tanks, all kinds of services including food

supply, ammunition supply, use of radio, signals and radar).
All such movements were directed to the defeat of imaginary
enemies. Realism was provided by using many other British
troops as fictitious Germans.

I remember those winter months as very cold, with much
snow and ice. Unlike the Germans and Russians, we did not
possess boots and clothing well adapted to the climate of
northern Europe. Perhaps this can be explained by the fact
that a large proportion of our small army had been stationed
in India, but in any event the British winter is usually less
severe than that of the northern plains of Europe. Anyway,
we built Nissen-hutted camps while shivering in bitter winds,
stood on parade in sleety slush with painfully cold feet, and
standing on sentry duty at night was itself an endurance test.

During the periods of movement intended to train the
staff, it was often impossible for soldiers, including most
junior officers, to be kept informed about what was supposed to be going on. Such unawareness has a demoralizing
effect, especially in what is known among trade unionists in
the building industry as 'inclement' weather.

A 'scheme' would run more or less as follows. A large
enemy force was supposed to have got ashore over a ten-
mile stretch south of Dunwich and was heading for Bury St
Edmonds. Our task was to sweep through the country from
north and south, intercept the force and split it into dis-
organized groups, each to be annihilated completely.

As we drove along the lanes, halting inexplicably at frequent intervals, we would hear gunfire but had no idea
whether the guns belonged to the enemy or ourselves. We
were supposed to be kept 'in the picture', but nobody in
sight knew what it was. We would stop about lunch time
and were hungry. Was there time to cook something?
Nobody knew. If the column stopped in the evening,
perhaps because of a broken bridge, how long would the

sappers take to mend it? Or, should we settle down for the night? Nobody knew. When at some stage we were ordered to sleep, we covered ourselves in groundsheets (often wet) and tried to snooze in the vehicles.

Just as we were dozing off we would hear a word of command: 'Prepare to move.' We responded with a string of expletives.

One very cold day in March, the company to which my section belonged (minus our vehicles) were told to get across a small river to avoid being cut off by the enemy. I was carrying an antitank rifle on my shoulder, a heavy, most clumsy thing it was. The river was partly covered with ice. I slipped down into the water and almost immediately found myself out of my depth. Struggling to keep the weapon out of the water, I managed to swim across the few yards to the other bank and to scramble ashore, and the other men followed.

Looking back, I noticed that the man following me was in a fainting condition. I dropped the big rifle, went back into the water and dragged the man ashore, hoisting him up by one of his arms. He fainted but soon recovered, though looking very pale. Leaving the rifle by the river, I carried the man to a nearby cottage and knocked on the door. Two women opened it. I asked if they could let me have a basin of hot water into which I could put the feet of my comrade, to revive him. The women helped me to remove the man's wet clothing and draped him in blankets. After about twenty minutes he was fully recovered. He dressed himself again (which could not have been a very enviable experience). I thanked the women and the two of us eventually reached our own platoon.

Three men were drowned in that river and there was a controversy about the wisdom of the kind of training that we had endured. I think that the merit of endurance tests is that they alone enable a human being to become aware of the extent of his own powers.

During a lull in these strenuosities, one of our officers raised the absorbing question of whether or not a Bren carrier would float or sink if driven into a river. Some, including myself, thought it was bound to sink and that, even if it did float, the engine would be flooded. And, even if the engine continued to work, the tracks would not make the craft navigable. Others were less pessimistic. To settle the matter the officer called for volunteer drivers prepared to drive their own machines into a certain river. Several men volunteered, including a man called Winter, a tall, blond, rather humorous fellow, whom the officer selected for the performance.

We stood and watched, some putting bets on the outcome. Winter started his engine and drove gently down into the stream. The vehicle sank down immediately, the engine stopped with a hiss of steam and Winter sat up to his waist in cold muddy water. A big crane had to be summoned from a nearby town to lift the machine out of the river, but I do not recall how, if at all, it was restored to working order. As for Winter himself, he acquired a nickname for his gallantry. Ever afterwards he was known as Able Seaman Winter.

I was posted to the officer cadet-training unit at Douglas in the Isle of Man in July 1942 and spent four months there till we were commissioned into various regiments late in November. Those four months were very memorable, largely because of the beauty of the island's landscape as it then was, almost devoid of tourists from the mainland. The Manx people had their land almost entirely to themselves.

I found myself in the company of forty or fifty other cadets, all formerly non-commissioned officers of all ranks and from many different British regiments. We all lived in the buildings of a private hotel on the seafront or promenade. The catering was provided by the owners of the hotel.

The promenade of Douglas is very long and stands high above the sea. Our buildings were situated at the southern end of the promenade, not far from the docks. To the north of us a long row of former holiday boarding houses had been commandeered by the British government to provide housing for hundreds of German and Italian internees for the duration of the war. All those buildings were enclosed in barbed wire with armed sentries at various points. Walking on the promenade we could watch these men as they did exercises to keep themselves fit, or gossiped in groups. I wondered about their thoughts and feelings.

On the other side of the island, at Port Erin, there was another camp for interned women, many of them being the wives of the men at Douglas. Several times a week, groups of wives under the supervision of an elderly British sergeant with a rifle over his shoulder would be brought by bus to Douglas to visit their languishing husbands behind the barbed wire entanglements. *Love Wired Up* or *Love with Barbed Wire* could be Booker titles for whatever presumably went on.

The amount of information, instruction and training packed into those four months was phenomenal, and I think that the most successful cadets were those best able to follow the detail of lectures, take notes and remember facts. In all this I was a very average achiever. I did best at map reading and sheer endurance tests not involving intelligence, such as marching across the island on an empty stomach (the hills are very steep) or climbing up a rope from the beach to the promenade carrying a Bren gun or rifle together with a weight over my shoulder representing the body of a comrade wounded in an imaginary battle. At field firing exercises an officer would yell at the top of his voice: 'Mortar bombs are falling all round this place. What are you going to DO?' I don't think I was particularly good at answering his question in the second permitted for the purpose.

Our principal lecturer was a captain with a Yorkshire accent and a marvellous sense of humour. Instructing us in the use of camouflage he suggested that vehicles could often be usefully camouflaged by smearing them all over with cow dung. If sufficient cow dung was not available, it had been found that bullshit was equally serviceable. He was very funny about latrines for troops. Trenches for that purpose should be very deep so that plenty of earth could be thrown into them every day. That would prevent flies from spreading infection, especially when the flies got browned off by the boredom of life down below. In the army everybody was 'browned off' by something or other.

A large proportion of the cadets had come from Scottish regiments. For historical reasons going back to the independence movements of the early eighteenth century, the Scottish cadets seemed to view the prospects of becoming officers as primarily a sartorial matter. During those months of my life I had never before heard so much talk and argument about tartans, troops, sporrans, dirks, badges and emblems. It was as though we were preparing for a hunt ball instead of a world war. For us Englishmen the outlook was darkened by the thought of enormous tailors' bills and the need for overdrafts, and we felt embarrassed by the oddity of being saluted by soldiers whenever we ventured into a street. While less obsessed with uniforms than the Scots, we may have been more inwardly concerned about the gravity of the war.

I recall a small incident in the course of our training at Douglas. One of the officers on the staff opened a lecture like this: 'As you know, in this period we are to learn about the XYZ antitank mine. Has anybody ever seen one?' One of the cadets raised his hand: 'Yes, Sir.' 'Well then,' said the officer: 'You can come up on this platform and give the lecture about it.' The cadet did his best to obey and we got some notion of the missing gadget, but I never afterwards beheld a real one. Recording this episode illustrates an implication of some of my work at PEP outlined in the chapter headed, 'At the start'.

Between 23 October and 4 November 1942 the battle of El Alamein took place. A special thanksgiving service was held in the Anglican church in Douglas and we cadets were paraded to participate in it. We marched through the streets in our Sunday best.

When I was within a few yards of the church door I heard an officer's voice shouting: 'Is Cadet Terrell there? Cadet Terrell!' I called out 'Sir!' The officer, our Yorkshire lecturer, rushed up to me and said: 'Cadet Terrell, you need not go in if you do not want to.' To which I replied: 'It's all right, Sir. I shall attend the service,' which I did.

That small incident affected me for the rest of the war. I was known as an 'agnostic', 'free thinker' or 'atheist' and had often wondered how, with my dubious attitude to the Almighty (if any) I could possibly conduct a church parade if I became an officer. Logically, I should decline to do so. But illogically I could, would and actually did so.

How could I justify my attitude? Each of us, during those years, pondered over the definition of his or her 'war aims'. When the officer told me that I need not attend the service unless I wanted to do so, his action expressed a respect for intellectual liberty. While sitting through the service in silence, I decided that my war aims must be to defend the kind of individual liberty that had just been bestowed on me.

* * *

The guise of a soldier, whatever his rank or expertise, implies the cultivation of certain attitudes and ways of looking at the physical world. Such attitudes (and aptitudes) are shared with animals. Waterfowl, for example, can be seen asleep with beaks tucked under wings at any time of day or night. A soldier, too, should be able to sleep for 20 minutes with similar readiness. Most animals survive without regular mealtimes, eating whenever an opportunity occurs. A soldier may have to behave likewise. Although never much of a soldier, I have always been able to sleep or eat to order.

Very early in my training I found myself, in any landscape, thinking about imaginary targets for attack or sites for defence. In peacetime, maps assist us in finding the way and imagining topographical features beyond our limited visual horizon. In war, they help to answer other questions: if I stood at point X, would I be visible by an enemy standing at position Y? If I am ordered to attack place P, should I approach it via Q or via R? Or (a common question in Burma) 'Can we cross that stream by wading across it, or must we swim or build a bridge?' Only gradually, after a war, do such states of mind dissolve.

4

To the Slave Coast

At the end of our training as cadets we were given a few days of leave before reporting to the commanding officers of the various regiments into which we had been commissioned. I went, of course, to London, to join my wife. She was then sharing a very small flat in West Hampstead with a bombed out couple. I slept on the floor in cramped conditions. We enjoyed ourselves, however, in the crowded bars and cafes of Soho, dancing and forgetting about bombs and broken glass, singing about the cliffs of Dover and using up food coupons.

I had been ordered to report to the CO of the 2nd Essex Regiment, then stationed at the famous old country house, The Grange near Alresford in Hampshire. Its fine panelled interior walls were boarded up and the great rooms (so suitable for a modern production of the Antiques' Road Show) were devoid of carpets and furniture. Men slept in rows on the ballroom floor. From across the valley below, The Grange resembled an outsize Greek temple, with owls and rooks beneath its crumbling roof and military trucks churning up its lawns. A fountain or two continued to play and ornamental fish could be glimpsed or guessed at.[*]

It was impossible adequately to heat the huge rooms with two or three flickering log fires. We lived all day in our over-

---

[*] There is much information about The Grange in Virginia Surtees's book *Jane Welsh Carlyle* (Michael Russell, 1986).

coats, often sitting on benches near a fire and trying to concentrate on a lecture by our old soldier commander about the pure theory of outposts in military tactics. The official handbooks seemed out of date, however recently printed.

One of my earliest actions after joining the Essex Regiment as a subaltern was to fill a notebook with descriptions of all the men in my platoon (about 26 of them). In this I was prompted by two factors. Most important was the general spirit of the cadet training centre in the Isle of Man, where much attention had been given to the responsibilities of officers for the welfare of their men. I should get to know every man by his name or nickname and be aware of the peculiarities of each. The other factor was my recollections of the personal problems of fellow recruits in the King's Royal Rifle Corps.

One of my men always walked or marched in a curious way, holding his right shoulder higher than his left and leaning his head to the right. When I asked him what he had done in 'civvy street' his reply explained his posture. He had been a furniture remover. For several years his job had consisted of moving pieces of furniture (for example, a wooden bench, a fender, a small cupboard) from a house to a lorry or vice versa — all such articles had been supported on his right shoulder, his head leaning towards them, his right hand raised to keep the thing in place.

Another man suffered acutely with a form of foot rot. His feet were always sore and the medical officer kept them bandaged. He had worked for several years in a fish shop. On his feet he had worn only thin, leaky patent leather shoes. Since the marble floor of the shop was frequently hosed down with cold water, his feet were always wet and, in winter, very cold. His employers had never thought of giving him gum boots nor, apparently, had it occurred to him to buy some, perhaps on credit.

I had toothache and, after some delay, was at last dealt with by the nearest dental medical officer, who gave me an excellent filling. I told him I had been horrified by the state of the teeth of many of the men in my own platoon. He explained to me that most poor people with toothache simply requested the dentist to extract them, because extractions were so much cheaper than fillings. An extraction cost only about 7s. 6d., but a filling could cost three guineas or more. He said that it was only since he had joined the army that he had been able to do any real dentistry.

During the following weeks we moved to various other sites in southern England, including camps in Hampshire and the Marlborough Downs. I did not much enjoy my spell with the Essex Regiment, missing the humour of my former London companions. My new officer colleagues seemed to me a solemn group of pseudo country gentlemen who disliked any kind of intellectual activity. To start a discussion, say, of Sir William Beveridge's proposals for a postwar welfare state was to invite a curt snub.

However, I did make quite close friends with two of my officer colleagues. One of them, a major and company commander, was knowledgeable about Japan and able to speak the language. He was tall, dark and slightly bald with a wavy moustache resembling that of the famous explorer of the previous century, Sir Richard Burton. He had also much experience of India, whether military or not, I cannot say.

I wondered what such a valuable man was supposed to be doing among the men of rural Essex at such a time. Should he not be teaching Japanese or otherwise contributing his knowledge to the war effort? I never questioned him about his prospective destiny, which seems a pity. At that time, when hundreds of men were waiting in camps all over Britain, individuals with special knowledge or experience seemed to be unnoticed by authority above. Many such men, including my Burtonish friend, never dreamt of putting themselves forward.

The other man whom I admired, differed so greatly from the explorer that he could only have originated on another planet. He was my own chief and company commander, a very handsome, blond, jolly fellow several years younger than myself. He was a captain with a picturesquely aristocratic manner. His principal concern was to go to bed with the most beautiful women for miles about, whom he met at local dances.

He used me as a sort of go-between. Very fond of the same women myself, I was expected to talk about him while dancing with them. I found little difficulty with this procedure, however, for such women had often noticed my handsome commander in the dance hall and questioned me about him. Anyway, sometimes in the early morning I would advise him to remove lipstick from his cheek before we went on parade.

The Essex Regiment consisted of what were called 'heavy' infantry. This created a minor but awkward difficulty for me. My former regiment, The Kings Royal Rifle Corps was, of course a 'rifle' regiment, As such, it was accustomed to marching at a very fast pace. That pace was never reduced, whatever the gradient of a road. The Essex men, by contrast, marched at the ordinary and relatively slow pace of most infantry, and always lowered the pace when ascending a hill. As a platoon commander, I was responsible for setting the pace of the column behind me.

I was several times severely rebuked for setting what was regarded as an outrageously fast pace on route marches. I would apologize, reduce the pace and very shortly commit the same offence again: a small matter that did not seem so small at the time. Life continues to be replete with dimensional inconsequentialities.

To the Slave Coast

* * *

One never knew from week to week what to expect. Suddenly, I was sent for by the commanding officer and told that I was to be posted abroad and would be given a few days of embarkation leave in London. During that spell of leave I was to purchase at a particular shop certain tropical clothing which made it clear that my destination was to be some part of West Africa. Life in those years was rather like the children's game of 'pass the parcel'. Whoever has the parcel when the music stops must open it and discover its only guessable contents.

After the busy spell of leave I had to go to a large building in the Marylebone Road (a commandeered hotel) known in military parlance as a 'transit camp'. It was crammed with British officers and soldiers of all kinds, all waiting to travel by road or train to ports of embarkation in convoys of ships destined for various parts of the world between the Caribbean and the Far East, all movements conducted in maximum secrecy. Most of us, I suppose, would during the previous few hours, have left the embraces of loved ones before departing into the unknown.

In the First World War men were destined for France, Flanders or the Middle East. In my war, there was more mystery and distances were immense. Eventually, I found myself in a troop train bound for Liverpool, in a compartment full of strangers whose talk included the occasional offer of a cigarette or an attempted joke.

* * *

At Liverpool, a large number of us boarded one of the old

Highland line ships, which, in peacetime, brought frozen meat and chilled citrus fruit from South Africa. It was called the *Highland Princess*, now painted grey all over. On board, were about a hundred British officers and several hundred British troops, most of them NCOs.

We formed part of a convoy of over forty vessels and, to avoid German submarines and possible air attacks, the convoy moved in a huge circle via the north Atlantic before sweeping down towards the West African coast. We were to call at Bathurst (in the Gambia), at Freetown (in Sierra Leone), at Takoradi (in the Gold Coast) and at Lagos (Nigeria). No man was told at which port he would be disembarking until an hour or two beforehand. A destroyer, moving always at great speed, weaved about among the ships of the convoy, prepared for battle at any moment. I remember being told how to operate an Oerlikon anti-aircraft gun, but doubt if I could actually have done so in an emergency.

Having travelled much by sea in the past, I was determined to treasure the visual experience again: the glorious clarity of the horizon in the early morning; romantic sunsets; schools of porpoises and leaping dolphins flashing in the sunlight; jellyfish moving gently in the breeze; translucent waves curving against the metal sides of the ship. Ship life was uncomfortable because there were virtually no chairs on deck. Bunks were cramped at night. The food was good, however.

One day, not far from Dakar there was a sudden alarm (I forget the signal for it). We donned our life jackets and helmets and went deliberately, without running, to the parts of the decks known as our 'action stations', there to await events. The sea was rough in brilliant sunshine, white surf in all directions. I remember the feeling of expectancy, the grim uncertainty: if a torpedo were to strike our ship there would

46

be a huge explosion, a heavy blow to one's head or body, a last glimpse, cold water — blackness.

Suddenly we heard another signal: 'Stand down' — the emergency was over — how we never knew. Was an enemy submarine destroyed by our own action? Had the alarm been a false one or just a training exercise? What lesson was to be learned? For me, it was not a practical matter such as 'Always do such and such. Never do X or Y.' Looking back I see it as an ingredient of war itself: the immediacy of the unknown.

On the same day we passed a light brown boat tossing helplessly in the waves. It resembled a lifeboat from a larger vessel. In it were the bodies of three men. Had they been killed by machine-gun fire from above, or had they died of thirst and exhaustion?

While we were anchored in the suffocating heat of Freetown harbour, we officers put on a variety show to entertain the men. I was asked if there was anything I could contribute. The only song whose words I could remember was that of the highwayman hero of John Gay's *The Beggar's Opera*, Captain Heath. In a dungeon with a ball and chain attached to his ankle, he waits to be hanged. He sings the famous air:

> *When the heart of a man is depressed by care*
> *The mists are dispelled when a woman appears.*
> *Like the notes of a fiddle she sweetly, sweetly*
> *Lightens our troubles and charms our ears.*
> *Roses and lilies her cheeks disclose*
> *And her ripe lips are more sweet than those.*
> *Press her, caress her with blisses — her kisses*
> *Dissolve us in pleasure and soft repose.*

I sang the song with near hysterical passion, for the air is superb. The men, who knew nothing of the opera, clapped a bit, but I felt that some other song would have been more appropriate.

Another officer pretended to be a striptease artiste who, appearing only as a shadow upon a white sheet, stripped slowly and seductively, wringing the sweat out of each garment in turn. His show seemed to combine striptease with laundry. The applause was immense.

After leaving Freetown harbour our ship broke away from the rest of the convoy, which headed south, round the Cape and up the East African coast, disembarking men at various ports before crossing the Indian Ocean to Bombay. Our ship moved along the West African coast to Takoradi and finally to Lagos, where the last of us, including myself, disembarked.

Disembarkation was for me sad, for the voyage along the famous Slave Coast had been so moving. Each day we had gazed at the coast, endless green undulating bushland, glimpses of lagoons, ancient fishing boats reminiscent of paintings by Van Gogh, great stretches of sand, white breakers rolling towards the shore. At night, small clusters of lights indicated thatched villages hidden beneath palms and trees. Sometimes we came close to a fishing boat whose African crew would wave and joke with us strangers in their ancient world. I thought how wonderful it would have been if we could have sailed on close to the Biafra shore, the Cameroons, the Congo and Angola. Little is known about the yearnings of men for particular images of the land and sea. Lapland and Greenland mean little to me; Malabar and the Carnatic — yes.

Before producing any more vignettes for this memoir, I shall now break off for an attempt to enlighten the reader about our military role.

To the Slave Coast

* * *

All of us in our ship, and in several other similar ships that reached the coast before and after ourselves, were destined greatly to strengthen the existing Royal West African Frontier Force (RWAFF), a miniature army that owed its origins to the so-called 'scramble for Africa' during the last two decades of the nineteenth century and the first few years of the twentieth. Its principal architect had been Captain F. D. Lugard (later Lord Lugard) (1858–1945), by far the most important figure in the history of British administration in East, central and West Africa.* The main objectives of Lugard's policies were first to put an end to the slave raiders and traders of East and central Africa and, in West Africa, to defend the various British spheres of interest and systems of government against the encroachments of other European powers, especially France and Germany.

Since the fall of France under the German onslaught of 1941, the large city and port of Dakar on the coast of French West Africa had become a German submarine base from which great damage had been inflicted upon British shipping in the Atlantic. Many of the ships linking Britain with South Africa and India had also been lost by torpedo attacks based on Dakar. The original purpose of strengthening the RWAFF had been to facilitate a military attack on Dakar from the Saharan hinterland. Before we had sailed from Liverpool, however, that objective had become

---

* Two books form the basic sources for Lugard's extraordinary career. First, his own *The Rise of our East African Empire* (2 vols 1893) and Margery Perham's standard biography (2 vols 1956 and 1960).

redundant. Inspired by the leadership of General de Gaulle, the French themselves recaptured Dakar for the new France.

The RWAFF seemed like an army dressed up with nowhere to go. But not for long. The French action at Dakar released our little army for transfer to India, whose eastern frontiers were now menaced by the Japanese.

5

Nigeria and beyond

We saw virtually nothing of the island and city of Lagos, for we immediately boarded a train for the interior. The journey was very slow through a steeply undulating landscape covered with dense vegetation, including thousands of tall palms and very tall trees valued for their hardwood timber. This region, the land of the Yoruba people, is the most densely populated in all Africa south of the Sahara. Years later, during my years at the old Colonial Office, I studied the causes of this. The soil is exceedingly fertile, which enables the people of many large towns to be amply supplied with food grown within walking distance of the inhabitants. During the eighteenth and nineteenth centuries, the people of the region had drawn together in what became towns for self defence against the Arab slave *raiders* from the north and the European slave *traders* from the sea.

Our train passed through much of this densely populated region from south to north. Whenever we stopped at a station the platforms were crowded with people of all ages, hundreds waving and cheering at the unfamiliar spectacle of so many white soldiers in their midst. None of us had expected such a reception, which affected our response to African people forever after.

I and many other officers and NCOs left the train at the Yoruba township of Ede (pronounced Eddé) and were taken in trucks to a large tented area containing various units of the new so-called 81st West African Division. I became a member of the 1st Sierra Leone Regiment. I shall not tax the reader with an account of the divisional structure. All of us wore on an upper arm a black and yellow picture of a most repulsive looking spider or tarantula. In West African fairy tales, spiders are somehow faithful allies of man. Scorpions, snakes and praying mantises are less well disposed.

We officers occupied low roofed brown tents, and I was lucky to have one of them to myself. We slept on very low camp beds. The soil was of reddish, gritty sand in which small scorpions seemed to be at ease. I was advised to shake out my boots carefully to eject scorpions before donning them in the early mornings.

I do not remember the name of our commanding officer, but he was an elderly man (perhaps about fifty) and seemed to have belonged to the Sierra Leone Regiment since his boyhood. I liked him at once. He introduced me to the men of my platoon in an extraordinary lingo, pidgin English.

In the regiments of northern Nigeria, where Hausa is the dominant language, officers were required to learn and speak it. However, it would have been impossible for the newly arrived officers from Britain, or new British NCOs to learn more than a smattering of Hausa during the rest of the war. And so far as Sierra Leone was concerned, it was not Hausa but a group of other languages that were spoken by the people anyway. There followed a wider use of pidgin throughout the RWAFF.

The Africans slept on closely packed bunks in marquees. African NCOs dealt with matters of discipline, drill and the control of troops. The British NCOs handled all the paperwork, supplies, stores and administrative details, which were considerable.

I was provided with a batman, a small, very loyal Muslim whose name was Fodi Sesay. His immediate action in emergencies was to bring me a mug of tea. He polished my boots to shop-window brilliance and spread out whatever garments were required and did my laundry. There was a small galvanized bath into which, every evening, Fodi would pour a few inches of sandy hot water for my ablutions. It was not his job, however, to remove very slow moving millipedes, grey in colour and entirely imperturbable.

Among our African NCOs was a Sergeant Johnson. Perhaps because of his English name he was automatically posted to the British sergeants' mess. He possessed what seemed to him to be a valid claim to British identity, for one of his thumbs was white. When challenged, he declared that his grandfather had been a European. The British sergeants supported his claim and kept him in their own mess.

The CO had at first wanted me to become a mortar officer, but that turned out to be impracticable because all the mortars of the division had already been sent down to Lagos to be shipped to India. So, apart from a little drill, numerous inspections, marches, firing practice on a shooting range, and some attempt to amuse the men at odd moments, I felt a bit up in the air. Occasionally, a man would rush up to me, salute smartly and say: 'Sir. Which time dis war done finish?' Some of the men sought my help in writing letters home. The role of an officer was that of what was known as a 'savvy man', someone who knew everything and provided information without payment

Part of my duties was the familiar task of looking into the feeding arrangements of the men. Almost at once I was shocked by the large number of complaints by men with 'belly palaver' (stomach ache) after meals.

It did not take me long to discover the cause of the trouble. All the men came from Sierra Leone, where the main bulk foods of the people consist of locally grown rice and cassava, a root crop, together with yams (large potato-like tubers). All these form easily digestible farinaceous food. But in Nigeria there was very little rice. There had, indeed, been a world shortage of it since the Japanese had been in control of the world's largest rice producing country, Burma. Most Nigerians ate locally grown millet, which grew abundantly on the land all round Ede. Millet, however, has exceedingly hard seeds, which can only be made digestible by hours of heavy pounding in wooden mortars. This work was done by the women of every village. After such pounding the grain was reduced almost to powder. It could then be stewed together with red palm oil, bits of meat and chillies pounded with rock salt. I discovered how the women of Ede and surrounding villages prepared the daily food by watching them and asking innumerable questions.

It seemed to me astonishing that, in our battalion we did not seem to have a single officer who knew or seemed to care how our own troops were fed. They looked upon me as a sentimental busybody. I looked upon them as unconscious racists. Anyway, I sought an appointment with our experienced and kindly CO and asked him if I might do various things to improve catering for the men. I wanted a lorry and a driver and a sum of money, say a couple of hundred pounds. I would go to the market at Ibadan, about seventy miles away, and buy a number of big wooden mortars, pestles and stone slabs with stone rolling pins for grinding up chillies with rock salt. The CO beamed. 'Yes, I'll give you all that. I had been wondering what the devil to do with you but, as from tomorrow I shall appoint you to a new job — African Chop and Welfare Officer. You can give all your attention to the chop business.'

On my return from Ibadan with a truck full of gear, I arranged for two separate stews to be cooked. One would be prepared exactly as heretofore; the other after two hours of pounding of millet and proper grinding of chillies with salt.

Each such stew would be eaten by a sample group of men (I forget how many). And so it was. After eating his meal, I ordered each man to go and sit down on the grass out of earshot of all the others. I then went to each man with my pencil and notebook. The conversations went like this:

Self: Corporal Momo!
Momo: Sir!
Self: Which chop you done eat?
Momo: De old one, Sir.
Self: You get belly trouble?
Momo: Yes, Sir.

The replies to the questionnaire showed conclusively that the men who had eaten the stew of my own recipe had enjoyed it with no belly palaver. I went in triumph to the CO and reported my findings. There followed a revolution in the diet of the battalion. More equipment was obtained from Ibadan and I gave a few demonstrations, with the aid of our cooks, to officers and men of other units in our brigade. I do not know what effects followed so far as they were concerned.

I did other things as well. Meat and yams had been hacked up and thrown into the stewing cauldrons without first being washed to remove grit, sand or mud. Gritty stew is not much fun, even for African consumers.

We remained at Ede for several weeks during which life was not dedicated exclusively to cooking. Sometimes, I took my platoon for a route march with a few little military exercises on the way, such as practising what to do in the event of a sudden attack from the air, or confronting an imaginary enemy tank. On such marches, it was customary for an officer to march well ahead of his troops — not, I thought, very sensible, for it made him conspicuous for no good military reason.

As we tramped along a hot, dusty road, sweating profusely, the men would start a song. Unbeknown to myself they had given me a nickname 'de Captain Cuss-cuss'. Cuss-cuss was the food made from cassava roots. They had promoted me to the rank of captain, though I was a mere second lieutenant.

Song on the march always took a particular form. A soloist and wit would start off by improvising a roughly rhythmic patter, reminiscent of the West Indian calypso. This was uttered in a mixture of pidgin English and one or other of the languages of Sierra Leone. Every now and then would come a refrain of two or three lines of catchy melody, everybody joining in. All I could hear of the solo were occasional references to cuss-cuss and chop, and frequent bursts of laughter. When I mentioned all this to colleagues in the mess, they laughed and told me that the men had been making fun of myself. They made similar fun of all the officers and liked to imitate their speech in a hoity-toity manner. Africans like a joke and seem to laugh more readily than other men. I discovered more of this later in the story.

Every now and then, in the cool of the evenings two or three trucks would set off for a neighbouring town, Oshogbo, which was bigger than Ede. Virtually all of us, including the officers, went to Oshogbo for women. For this purpose, the Africans were ingenious. Making friends with women in the town they got them to put on spare military uniforms and travel back to Ede in the trucks. We pretended not to notice, but I remember my surprise on noticing the earrings and necklaces of the supposed soldiers. I felt sorry for those women and wondered how they managed to get back to Oshogbo with pockets full of cash.

As for the officers, our destination in Oshogbo was the Syrian Club, where, at the bar, we could eat delicious cold chicken and drink rice beer imported from the Congo.

Somewhere behind curtains we could dance with beautifully dressed African women and go to bed with them too. Plonky music came out of a gramophone. Mutual affection was evident and genuine

Our excellent CO did not accompany us to India but remained in Nigeria, presumably to help with the formation of the 82nd Division, which eventually followed us. I do not recall how it occurred, but I was somehow ordered to continue to supervise the cooking on the ship, which was another of the old Highland line vessels. This meant taking with us all the pestles, mortars and other gear from the camp.

Since we expected to round the Cape in the middle of the southern winter, all the men at Ede were issued with warm, British style uniforms, woolly vests, warm shirts and long underpants. I remember conducting a morning kit inspection to ensure that every man was in possession of the requisite gear. Many men were unable to display particular items. I would say to a man: 'Which side you done put your vest?' The reply would be: 'E done lost, Sir!' Later, walking in the streets of Ede I would notice civilian Africans wearing woollen vests and long pants, all sweating profusely. Our troops were not averse to selling their new clothes for ready cash. West Africans of both sexes are instinctive traders. What could we do about it?

For stewing food for African troops the ship had been fitted with six electrically heated cauldrons, similar in appearance to the 'coppers' in which clothes were washed long ago. Three of them were situated on the bow deck and the other three astern. I immediately set about organizing parties for such tasks as bringing up sacks of food from the hold, pounding millet, opening cans of corned beef and big cans of palm oil to ensure that all aboard would be fed before darkness fell. The only meat for the rest of the voyage would be corned beef. All seemed to be going well when the ship sailed with great wavings to loved ones left ashore. I was too busy to join in this.

After we had been at sea for a couple of days — again as part of a large convoy — all three of the cauldrons at the stern end broke down and nobody aboard was able to do anything about it. At first we assumed that the cauldrons would be put right at Cape Town, but that, too, proved to be impossible. So we travelled all the way to Bombay (two months at sea) entirely dependent on the three cauldrons at the bows. This meant cooking in shifts almost continuously all day and for much of the night. For me, at any rate, it was one of the most strenuous experiences of my war. Sometimes I lay at night wondering what would happen if our only remaining cauldrons were to break down as the others had done. Presumably, the entire convoy would have been obliged to stop, a difficult and dangerous operation. All the troops in our ship would have to be taken in rubber dinghies and distributed among all the ships bound for Bombay. After leaving Cape Town the convoy would be divided between ships bound for East African ports and the rest going to Bombay. In retrospect, I suppose that a lesson to be learned was that, if something awful might occur, try singing another song.

A few days before we reached Cape Town our new CO (Lieutenant-Colonel Carter) delivered a lecture to all British officers and NCOs about the situation confronting us there. He warned us gravely against having anything to do with African women in the city. To avoid brawls and 'incidents' at a time when the harbour was full of troopships, the local authorities had enacted regulations imposing mandatory punishments (including imprisonment), upon members of local forces and upon members of visiting forces from all other parts of the British Empire, who might be convicted of having sexual relationships with women not of their own races. Most of us were vaguely aware of such regulations, but the lecture was wisely delivered.

It was somehow agreed with the shore authorities that our officers and NCOs should take small parties of African troops for walks in the city during the five days of our stay. Africans were hugely entertained by riding up and down in the lifts of tall buildings and department stores. For most of them, their previous lives as rural peasants had presented no such joys. I think local white people in Cape Town, whose experience of any other parts of the continent was limited, were astonished by the physique of our troops, especially the tall, powerful men of northern Nigeria, or broad hefty men from some of the southern districts.

In Cape Town, an idea occurred to me. During the voyage from Lagos the men had had no fresh fruit or vegetables. The ship contained refrigeration equipment. I asked the CO if I might purchase on shore a stock of fresh cauliflowers and cabbages, and enough fruit to enable every man to have an apple and an orange every day till we reached Bombay. Arithmeticians were engaged to make calculations and my suggestion was accepted in full.

And so we sailed on. For several successive days life aboard the troopship was very cold and the sea rough. I and many others were horribly sick. Many Africans professed to be able to defeat seasickness by chewing raw chillies, which they did with the aid of relatively non-inflammable tongues. I wonder what truth there was in their claims. Experts are seldom on the appropriate spot at any moment.

The men wrapped themselves in everything warm that they could lay hands on. How those who had sold their long johns in Ede managed I do not know. African sergeants would form their men up in lines on the deck and get a song going. One of them went like this:

Home again!
Home again!
When shall I see my home?
When shall I see my native land!
I never forget my home!

Over and over again. Another song included these words:

On de bank of Moa River
On de bank of Moa River
I see you tonight
When de moon shinin' bright
On de bank of Moa River.

Moa River is a real stream in Sierra Leone. Perhaps some African Vera Lynn was responsible for the song.

Since marching on deck was not possible, the men marked time — left right, left right, left right to the rhythm of their songs. Thus they coped with the cold.

* * *

I have been exceptionally fortunate in having travelled widely by sea in the north and south Atlantic, the Indian Ocean, the Black Sea and the Pacific. For reasons real and imaginary, my favourite ocean is the Indian one. It can be very rough, very calm, very hot and quite cold, depending on the season. Whenever I think of it, however, I see clouds rising in a huge arc across the sky, edged with silver and gold. The clouds, vast, dark cumuli, flash with forked lightning, silent and menacing before thunder rolls.

At some stage during the long voyage to Bombay, I was asked by the CO to take on the job of 'Current Affairs

Officer' for the troops on board. For this purpose I was allotted a largish room with a blackboard and various short brochures produced by the War Office. The brochures or pamphlets were intended to assist officers to explain to British troops what the war was about, and to elucidate situations in particular parts of the world. It was clear that such aids were of little use for myself, so I decided to talk to the troops about other matters. Current affairs, for them, could be interpreted as lessons in certain kinds of general knowledge. We were travelling for thousands of miles round the surface of the globe. So I told them about the planet, about the solar system and the other planets, and the relationship between earth and the moon. I told them about the distribution of the different kinds of human beings: the black people of Africa, the white people of Europe, the brown ones of south Asia and the yellow ones of the Far East, and how we would be going to war with some of them, the Japanese, who lived far away.

I had also been a current affairs officer with British troops in Britain. Whereas British troops, with few exceptions, regarded 'current affairs' as just another boring parade, Africans regarded lectures about them as a real treat. After a lecture, most British troops sat glumly waiting to be dismissed. Africans put up their hands to ask innumerable questions. My audiences were voluntary pupils, not troops on parade, and they were enthusiastic in the pursuit of general knowledge about the cosmos. Years later, when as a member of the old Colonial Office I visited schools in Nigeria, I found that African children loved going to school, and that there was very little truancy. That cannot be said of many British children, then or now.

1. ABOVE. Advancing along a "chaung" or dried up stream bed. A party led by a British NCO.

2. RIGHT. A typical scene in country described on our maps as "dense mixed jungle, mainly bamboo".

3. Making a "basha" with split bamboos.

4. ABOVE. Friendly Khumi tribesmen making bamboo rafts for transporting supplies down the Kaladan river and its tributaries.

5. BELOW. Khumi tribesmen carrying wounded West Africans to safety.

6. LEFT. Unarmed carriers bringing supplies from Chiringa.

7. BELOW. A brown bullock arriving by air from India. Most of the bullocks were white and humped, from the Punjab.

6

The impact of India

Despite some familiarity with the historical meaning of Bombay in our ancient links with the subcontinent, and recent memories of my father's talk of India, I was now to see the country for the first time. Hitherto, India had emerged from his letters, from press cuttings and books. The mere word 'India' implied the word 'problem'. Problems of diarchy, reserved seats and constitutions, all in a whiteness of cotton and a sheen of brown.

Of our arrival and disembarkation, my memory is concentrated on our march from the dockside to Victoria station in hot sunshine. We were smartly dressed in dark green denims with wide cowboy-like greenish hats. I cannot remember whether or not the men carried rifles or whether we officers had Sten guns or pistols. Anyway, we intended to make an impression by smartness of bearing and good marching. The streets had been cleared of traffic and dense crowds watched. As we marched, I felt, I still think, that civilian India was living in a peace of the previous half century, surrounded by a world war of which the bulk of its inhabitants were oblivious. Sheltered beneath their mountains, the civilians of India talked the politics of the past.

What could our troops have made of the strange world now pressing upon them as they marched? All the basic Indian realities of caste, religion, notions of power, diet, holiness, poverty and cruelty, lay beyond African awareness. The evidence that I can bring to my question is retrospective, predominantly visual and belongs to subsequent weeks. For security reasons, we were obliged to read the men's letters home to ensure that they contained no information that could be useful to an enemy. Many men mentioned the smallness of most Indians, the beauty of the women ('India woman like angel') and a curious point about clothing. Many Africans thought that Indian men and women dressed alike. Such a notion was new to me. The sari and the *dhoti* are very dissimilar, and no man would wear gold or silver sandals even in a rickshaw.

Our train journey took us in an easterly direction through suburbs of Bombay to Igatpuri at the foot of the Western Ghats. Thence the train zigzagged up forested slopes in which occasionally could be seen waterfalls vanishing into rocky jungle, scenes reminiscent of old engravings of mountain landscapes in the Alps, with palms instead of firs. Eventually, we reached open grasslands dominated by towering rocky peaks, some surmounted by the remains of old Maratha forts. This was the region of the ancient city of Nasik. Our destination was another town, Deolali, where the train stopped. Nearby, over miles of grassland and farming country, stood line upon line of tents and marquees stretching almost to the horizon. I do not recall how we reached the tents allocated to ourselves, but assume that we would have been transported gradually in relays of trucks, with our very considerable baggage.

We were now in one of India's largest military concentration and training areas. Within such a vast assemblage of forces were hundreds of separate units of British and Indian troops in which men were surrounded by their own kind, yet within sight of troops from all over India, each with their own language, religion, domestic customs and ancient history. I tried to imagine the staff work, presumably at New Delhi, responsible for the organization as a whole, its grand objectives and contingency plans for war both in the Middle East and on the frontiers of Burma and Malaya. Armies are large or small, but whatever their size, locked within each are troops who can never possibly envisage the whole of which they form a tiny part. Throughout my war I was intermittently aware of this, but never more than here in the great camp at Deolali.

At the time of our arrival in India in the summer of 1943, the full effect of the Japanese conquest of Burma, which deprived India of a major source of rice, was being felt. Hungry people could be seen everywhere. To relieve the situation a little, the commanders of all troopships arriving at Bombay were required to bring ashore with them as much as possible of any food remaining in their holds. We brought up to Deolali many sacks of Nigerian groundnuts, which turned out to be so infested with weevils that I could only burn all the sacks in a horrible bonfire. Our stocks of millet, chillies and a limited quantity of rice, were still fresh. The troops were dependent upon these supplies for several days during which our culinary destiny was transformed.

The food situation in India was too complicated to be described adequately in this memoir. However, the hero of the day was the new viceroy, Lord Wavell, who arrived in New Delhi in August 1943. Within a few days, he visited Calcutta and starving Bengal, where perhaps a million civilians had died. His basic measures were to place the distribution of rice in the hands of the Royal Indian Army Service Corps, the rapid introduction of a simple form of rationing in the most needy parts of the country, and the appointment of the most able R. G. Casey as governor of Bengal.

The Indian military authorities had no choice but to treat us as though we were Indian troops of a sort, however odd our appearance, physical and sartorial. We were therefore issued with such items as chapatti irons, sacks of wheat flour from the Punjab, sacks of raw turmeric root, sacks of raw ginger, of small Indian chillies and rock salt, even cardamoms, large saucepans, big cans of ghee (buffalo milk fat) and sacks of various lentils (dahl) and other forgotten mysteries. I do not think that a single one of our officers had the faintest notion of what might be achieved with all this stuff.

One thing was clear, at least to myself. We must learn at once how to make an eatable curry for a battalion of Africans in one go.

About half a mile from our camp was a large, beautifully equipped camp containing several thousand Madrassi Tamils who were being trained as drivers for the Royal Indian Army Service Corps. They were vegetarian Hindus.

I asked one of our senior officers if he would kindly approach one of the officers of the Madrassis and prepare the way for me to go with a party of our African cooks to learn as quickly as possible how to use the equipment and supplies in our possession. This was readily achieved. We found the Indian cooks most helpful, most of them being able to speak quite good English. Most interesting was the procedure for making chapattis with flour and ghee, rolling them into shape and flinging them down upon the curved iron, heated by burning charcoal; it was all very ancient. After that experience of so long ago I can never eat at an Indian restaurant without recalling those days with the Tamil cooks in their big corrugated iron cookhouse, and visits to their godowns redolent of spices and warm flour. Our cooks learned readily enough, and again there were demonstrations, questions, tastings and jokes. I recall the sensory world of it, but little of the detail.

Our nearest town of some size was Nasik, situated on an upper reach of the holy Godavari River, which flows right across India to the sea in the Bay of Bengal. The monsoon had several weeks yet to run, so the river was turbulent, swirling and yellow with sand and eroded limestone grit. The scene resembled a miniature Grand Canyon. At various levels, carved directly in the rock face, could be seen ancient figures of the symbolical divinities, Shiva and his consort Parvati, Rama and Sita, Ganesh, Vishnu, Krishna with his flute and the lovely Gopis. Not far away, also were the Pandulena caves in a pyramidical hillside, containing the mysterious figures of Mahayana Buddhism.

My interest in all this was stimulated by visits to the cinema in Nasik. The most popular Indian films consisted of ingenious representations of mythical stories from the classic epics of Indian antiquity. During the 1930s, the Indian film industry (the world's largest), had been revolutionized by Jewish refugees from the famous German film industry of Berlin, who made use of European musical instruments for the performance of purely Indian airs and rhythmic tunes. Indian musical instruments, though subtle and melodious, did not produce a sufficient volume of sound for effective use in a cinema containing hundreds of seats. All this made the acquisition of some comprehension of traditional social values more attainable by newcomers from the outside world than would otherwise have been possible.

During visits to the cinema, I noticed many of our troops among the audience. However ignorant any of us were of Hindi and Mahrathi, we picked up the tunes. Back in camp I often heard Africans singing the songs, using the Indian words for their sound alone.

I pondered about the problems of Indian nationalism in a society of mutually conflicting values and traditional ways of life, especially among the peasantry and the urban poor. How could any Western notion of nationalism be expected to embrace the values of Islam together with those of the Ramayana or Buddhist codes? And what place could any kind of socialism have in such a mix? Britain could only govern India so long as British administrators stood apart from every Indian mystery. Memories of my father and of fellow Indian students in London predisposed me to consider these things. I could share none of these concerns with any of my fellow officers. Good men, they seemed to me oblivious of the world about us.

A friendly Indian in Nasik suggested that I should pay a visit to Trimbak, a place of pilgrimage about fifty miles to the north. For that purpose I was allowed to use an old 'Indian' motorbike, and devoted a whole Sunday to the trip. The road, all the way, was a dusty, potholed lane passing through miles of farmland with patches of millet of various kinds, sugar cane, dahl and rice.

Trimbak itself, I remember as a little lost town surrounded by hills and rocky ledges. On those ledges were several small caves, some of them with metal bars to prevent entry and possibly exit too. Inside some of the caves sat holy beggars, supposed to survive exclusively upon such food and coins as they received from a devout public. Most holy men's foreheads were daubed with yellow paint or paint of other garish hues.

In versions of Hindu ethical philosophy, every man is destined to assume various roles in the course of life: lover, parent, worker, sage and holy beggar. In one street, I passed a row of several naked men squatting, some of them in possession of remarkable penises, all displayed for public admiration. Whether or not they were entitled to make any special use of their enviable members, perhaps on Sundays, I did not feel able to inquire. In matters of holiness, one takes things for granted, none the wiser.

I valued my visit to Trimbak because the aspect of the place was evidently very ancient indeed. If any of Alexander the Great's companions had visited it in the late fourth century BC, would they have seen a similar group of holy old codgers in caves? One of the gratifications of visiting India, or writing about it, is that anything one can recall is unlikely to become wholly out of date. In Trimbak I managed to eat an excellent curry lunch.

The journey back to Deolali was troublesome, partly because bumping over a thousand potholes made my back ache, and because the engine frequently stopped. Repeated kick-starts were pretty exhausting.

One feature of our camp at Deolali was horribly reportable. While the entire land area had been taken over by the military authorities, for some reason dozens of donkeys belonging to Indian farmers were free to graze in the camp area and roam all over it. Like other mammalian creatures, the donkeys discharged great quantities of urine and never hesitated to defecate without notice. The entire camp area stank abominably and was buzzing with flies. On one occasion, I returned from Nasik to find a donkey in my tent, which had defecated abundantly on my bed. Furious, I drove the creature out and away, flung all the bedding out of the tent and lay exhausted on the metal slats of the bed. I spent half the next morning, helped by Fodi Sesay, washing bedding and draping it over the tent to dry in the sun. It was my fault. I should have closed the tent more firmly.

At Deolali I suffered a mild attack of dysentery. Our medical officer put me in a truck and sent me to the British military hospital at Poona, where I received injections of some antibiotic drug and recovered after a few days of treatment. I was asked by a Eurasian sister if I could play chess. I said that I did know how to play, though not to the extent of actually winning a game. She asked the question because there was an American officer in another ward who would be very glad of a game. I went and introduced myself to him. Before we started to play, he told me his story. He belonged to an American division also stationed in the Nasik area. Months before, he had left San Francisco in a troop-ship bound for Hobart, Tasmania. After several days there, he had travelled in another troopship all the way to Colombo and at last to Bombay. There, like myself, he had travelled up through the Western Ghats to Deolali.

Dismounting from the train at night he had stumbled into a deep ditch and put his left knee out of joint. In great pain, he had been sent straight to the hospital in Poona where he had lain for several weeks, his knee swollen and painful. At one stage the authorities had prescribed a kind of physio-therapy that involved standing on his good leg and gently moving the bad one. The instructor, however, had ordered him to stand on the bad leg and wave the good one. When he attempted to do so he had collapsed in agony. He was due to be shipped back to San Francisco for demobilization in the near future. He did, however, win the game of chess.

7

A new job

In August or September 1943, towards the end of the monsoon, a messenger arrived at my tent with orders that I should report at once to the chief operational staff officer at divisional headquarters, about half a mile away from our part of the camp. He, a lieutenant-colonel, was known as 'the G1'. Ushered into his presence, very near to that of the general himself, whom I had never seen,* I saluted and was invited to sit down. On the other side of a table sat a lean, wiry, rather severe looking man. He was dark and did not look as though he found it very easy to smile. Although he became my boss, from that moment until the beginning of the following monsoon in June 1944, I have forgotten his name. Perhaps it is not unusual to forget the name of anybody of whom one feels a bit afraid. However, I do not anticipate a need to refer to him much in these pages.

He began by saying that, while my attention to the catering of the Sierra Leone troops had been appreciated, the need for such work would come to an end as soon as we moved into the forward areas. Catering for the troops would then be much simplified, with only a minimum of cooking in

---

* Major-General C. G. Woolner CB, CBE, MC. He was a sapper (engineer) general with long previous associations with West African troops. I remember him as being always immaculately dressed, never unshaven and a seemingly stern disciplinarian.

71

the field. The general had decided that a junior staff job would be suitable for me. Henceforth, I would belong to divisional headquarters and would hold the position of 'liaison officer', with the rank of lieutenant. The division consisted of two brigades of infantry, known as numbers five and six brigade. Number five brigade included three battalions of Gold Coast troops. Number six brigade included two battalions of Nigerians, the first battalion of men from Sierra Leone, plus a single company of Gambians.

What did 'liaison' mean, exactly? A divisional headquarters had to be situated at some spot away from the fighting troops and, in the country for which we were heading, our headquarters might be in a clearing surrounded by dense jungle half way up some mountainside. Liaison meant keeping the general and the operational staff informed about what was happening from day to day (or from moment to moment) to the various bodies of troops in the forward areas, on the flanks and even far to the rear. My job would involve taking orders to specific troops or getting the answers to special questions. A typical question might be: X battalion is situated on that hill. It may be cold up there. Can the men sleep without blankets? Find out as soon as possible. Or, the map shows a track leading out of that valley and over that hill. Could a column of men walk along it? If so, are there any obstacles to clear out of the way? Find out as quickly as possible.

While some questions could be dealt with by radio, many could not, and in such cases only personal contacts could be employed. If, in some circumstances, a liaison officer were to fall into a ditch, have a broken ankle or get shot, the general's question might never be answered at all. For practical and security reasons, all my work would be conducted on an oral basis. If I were captured the enemy would discover no papers to show what I was up to.

A *new job*

I think the new job was right for me, though it did not seem a particularly military one. An ordinary platoon commander imagines himself leading his men into battle. As a liaison officer, I should be very solitary, leading nobody. From now on I was to be a sort of observer sharing much in common with press reporters, who wore quasi-military uniforms. There were times, too, when I felt like an anthropologist in disguise.

We two liaison officers for the two brigades of the division were immediately responsible to a chief liaison officer who, in turn was under the command of the chief operational staff officer, who had interviewed me at Deolali. He was Captain Gerry Read, a very sweet natured man (who had been a young bank manager before the war). Whatever the weather or the austerity of our lives, his attire and personal grooming, like that of General Woolner, was always immaculate. I could always imagine what kind of bedside manner he would have adopted in an interview with a Kensington lady about her overdraft.

✳ ✳ ✳

When the time came for us to entrain for Calcutta I was put in charge of the divisional baggage and the miscellaneous African troops associated with the various parts of the headquarters, including clerks, servants, radio operators, typists and messengers, over a hundred men in all. I was to see that every item of baggage and every man was put aboard the train, and transferred to the ship to cross the bay to Chittagong. At that port I was to transfer everything and every man to a train on the dockside that would take us to the railhead at Dohazari in the foothills of the Arakan. The baggage was a mixture of items including heavy typewriters, duplicators, loads of paper, wireless sets, a few Bren guns, boxes of ammunition, suitcases, cans of foodstuffs and rolls of telephone cable. The baggage was put into special vans on the train and the troops into following coaches. All the rest of the train was crammed with civilians.

Views from the train brought back feelings similar to those experienced during our first few weeks in India. As we rumbled across an iron bridge above a small river, we could look down at women washing clothes, beating them against rocks, others cleaning brass bowls with sand and water until they gleamed in the sun; women were walking sedately with brass bowls on their heads, one arm akimbo; an old man was at prayer by the waterside; and children were splashing, their naked bodies shining wet. All clothing, every little gesture, seemed archetypal, ancient, beyond any distant war.

Then, there was the continuing famine. At every station, hungry children held up their hands to us, mimicking the act of eating, imploring us for food. Some of the troops opened cans of corned beef and gave them to the children. As vegetarians they could not eat such food and would rather die than do so.

At Calcutta, we spent a night in tents set up for us by Indian forces, and the next day we were taken, with the baggage, in trucks to the ship for loading and embarkation. My next clear recollection is of our arrival at nightfall at the dockside at Chittagong. There had recently been a minor Japanese air raid on the docks, though I could see no sign of damage. We had arrived deliberately at nightfall, in blackout conditions, in order to load the train under cover of darkness. A dockside crane was used for transferring the baggage from the ship to the docks, but everything had to be lifted on to the train by hand. For that purpose, an Indian officer had engaged about a hundred coolies who were placed at my disposal.

A *new job*

In a few minutes it became clear that the coolies were so emaciated by the famine that they could not lift most of the baggage at all. I dismissed them and ordered the African HQ troops on the ship to do the work under one of their own sergeants. They jumped to it with a splendid determination to show their strength. We completed the job before dawn, when I ordered a break for tea and biscuits, prepared by one of our cooks on the dockside.

During the night, as they heaved baggage on to the train, the troops sang songs from the Indian films we had seen at Nasik. Tired and hungry after a sleepless, strenuous night, we looked forward to some kind of respite as the train moved into the early morning stillness of Bengal. An horizon of jungle covered hills rose in white, filmy mist. Rising through the mist could be seen small columns of smoke from the cooking fires of thatched villages, each column vertical in the windless air.

Although Dohazari is only about thirty miles from Chitta-gong, the train moved very slowly, so I arranged for it to stop at a village siding for an hour or so for a makeshift breakfast and rest. Breakfast consisted, I vaguely remember, of tea, rice with Carnation milk and something sweet, probably canned Australian jam. The air was cool enough to enable all of us to lie in the shade of the train itself.

During this rest I heard a faint cry coming from some-where only a few yards from the rail embankment. I walked towards a clump of bamboo beneath which lay a small child, evidently abandoned to die of starvation. I picked it up, brought it back to the train and told an African to mix together in a mug a little warm, squashed rice with some Carnation milk and water, and to bring me a spoon. I managed to spoon several tiny quantities of the mixture into the little boy's mouth and was glad to see that he could really eat them. As I did so, a group of solemn villagers

75

gathered round, staring silently. I must do something quickly about the child. Looking at the villagers I carried it directly to a strong looking man. With a gesture of my arms, I made it clear that I was ordering him to find a way of looking after the child and placed it firmly in his arms. Several of the villagers murmured their approval in words I could not understand. Nobody spoke English in such a place. I turned to the men, ordered them back into the train and told the driver to get on to Dohazari. Were the parents of the child living? What became of that tiny boy?

In the Arakan, a steep ridge called the Mayu range formed a natural frontier. On the ridge was a large force of Indo-British troops, with artillery and most other arms. So long as they remained on the ridge, the Japanese could not attack them from the east with much confidence. Our role was, first, starting from our forward base at Chiringa, due south of Dohazari, to cross the hills to the east and descend to the valley of the Kaladan River at Daletme.

We were to advance down both banks of the river, which flowed southwards many miles to the east of the Mayu range, getting as far as possible towards the port of Akyab. Throughout, we should be operating in thinly held Japanese territory. In this way, we were to form an easterly shield for the Indo-British force on the range. During most of our campaign we found ourselves in a no-man's land. Spooky and frightening as it was, the whole experience was scenically superb. Much of what follows is intended to illuminate it with episodes remembered. So long as the reader can envisage the scenic background, chronology is of little account.

8

On the ground

Hitherto I have described my role more or less as it was outlined to me in advance at Deolali on the other side of India. We were now about to move into the forward area, much closer to enemy-held territory.

In this chapter I have confined myself to such recollections as seem to be correct, omitting many facts that I have forgotten, sometimes rather inexplicably. For example, on leaving the railhead at Dohazari and guided by two or three of our own officers who had come to meet the train, we marched about thirty miles due south to the area of a village called Chiringa, which was being established as our forward headquarters. We must have bivouacked in the open paddy fields beneath the stars, but I have no recollection of that experience at all, and I have only a hazy memory of our camp at Chiringa as it then was. I have a much clearer recollection of it as we found it on our return to it months later at the end of our campaign. However, I do recall the excellent trench latrines that had been prepared by an advance party, and finding myself again in the company of hundreds of our own troops.

While in western India I had had a lot to do with catering for the men. I can remember very little of our way of life after our arrival at Chiringa. Did we live in bamboo hutments or were our dwellings of corrugated iron with woodwork and cement floors. I cannot remember now. I know, however, that at that time and for months afterwards, we ate a vast amount of corned beef and biscuits, boiled rice, Australian porridge for breakfast, dried onions and endless mugs of hot sweet tea, very strong. I remember also a lot of soya bean sausages and canned bacon, plus plenty of hard dark chocolate. In the early days, such supplies reached us on the heads of the two auxiliary groups of unarmed carriers. Later on, in the jungle clad hills, supplies descended upon us by parachutes carried in Dakota aircraft from India. We ate a lot of cold food, but such heating as was necessary was achieved with the aid of military spirit stoves operated in ways similar to the old Primus stoves. Fires were avoided because rising smoke could reveal our whereabouts.

* * *

There was one aspect of our life in the country described on our maps as 'dense mixed jungle, mainly bamboo' that I must explain to the reader. It was a life of almost constant movement involving everybody from the general (General Woolner) himself down to the private soldier. We seldom occupied any position for more than a few days at a stretch.

Every military unit, large or small, has its own head-quarters, by which I mean the area on the ground occupied by its commander and his immediate staff of assistants, whatever their ranks and jobs may be.

In the ever-shifting tactical situations of any kind of warfare, efficiency is very dependent upon the speed and ease of communications between as many as possible of the various headquarters involved, whether by telephone, radio, physical mobility by transport involving aircraft, motor driven vehicles or simple footwork. Much of our training in the jungly and rainy country of the Western Ghats before we travelled by train across the subcontinent towards Burma, had consisted of setting up a divisional headquarters area as quickly as possible at any particular spot and shifting the whole affair to some other position a few miles away.

To achieve this, a sort drill was practised. The general and his ADC and messengers would always be in position X; the director of medical services would always be found at Y; the operational staff would always be at Z. The director of ordinance (artillery) would always be at Q; service corps must be located at R; signals at S; the padre could be contacted at T, and so on. And so, if I had been walking on my own for several days along tracks in the hills and was returning to a new headquarters area, I could always find my way to the spot, in which I could meet the G1 or his deputy. The same signposts could always be used, whoever might require them.

* * *

Perhaps the most important feature of our daily living conditions was the adaptability of West Africans themselves to the jungle about them.

The jungles of the world vary considerably in vegetation and terrain, but all have features in common, whether in the basin of the Amazon, the coastal regions of West Africa or the hills and mountains of Southeast Asia: abundant but seasonal rainfall, very fertile soil, abundant bamboo and the prevalence of many creepers hanging from the taller trees or spreading like ivy over the ground.

In such conditions, small groups of human beings are able to survive with a few domestic animals in little clearings linked together by well-trodden footways, but frequently with no wheeled transport. Dwellings are usually assembled rapidly with the use of split or round lengths of bamboo, bound together by creepers. These were known to the West Africans as 'tie-tie' and were often quite as strong as the strongest hempen string. Most serviceable furniture could be put together by the same means.

We never lacked benches, tables and chairs and the simple frames over which mosquito nets could be spread, surmounted by waterproof sheets in rainy conditions. Tall bamboos stuck into the ground could be made to form the walls of the various offices of a divisional headquarters. Finally, anywhere in such a territory, the masses of dead bamboo leaves can be heaped beneath a mosquito net to form a most comfortable mattress. As I write this paragraph I recall a frequent nocturnal experience, a heavy shower of rain with lightning and claps of thunder. There would come a moment, always anticipated, when a trickle of water seeped through the bamboo leaves into one's bed and thence through one's tunic and shirt to some helpless part of one's person. No remedy was ever available as thunder crashed and rumbled in the invisible hills. With the early morning sun all was again dry.

We, of course, were not the only military inhabitants of the Southeast Asian jungles in those years. Japanese, Indians, British and American forces also managed somehow. Perhaps a few of my readers who belonged to such forces will be prompted to explain how they too managed to survive.

9

The scene recalled

I now look back upon our long spell in the hills as a collection of mutually isolated incidents, each printed in memory but not in strict chronological order. And many of the most vivid images were not of an intrinsically warlike nature. Here are a few sequences selected at random.

During our march from Dohazari to Chiringa, I led a group of about thirty headquarters troops along a track that wound through a copse of trees about the size of those in a European orchard but, I think, with darker leaves. I soon noticed that several of the men had left the column and were hacking at the dark green bark of the trees with their machetes. They were stuffing loose bark into their packs as though they valued it for some reason. I called them back into line and asked what they had been doing. Some of them said good-naturedly: 'Sir! We savvy dis tree for we own country. E fine fine ting for fever.'

I later discovered that the trees were of the cinchona species whose bark when chewed yields quinine. The tree occurs in several parts of the world, including the West African rainforests. Its value as a remedy for fever must have been known to the people for ages before it was produced industrially in the Western world. On another occasion, I recognized the strong smell of wormwood and traced it to a large bush whose dark green leaves resembled laurel. Wormwood is the source of absinthe.

While all my walks in the hills had a military purpose —

to deliver orders or collect information from the various units of the sixth brigade, they often brought me into contact with the local people, the Kumis who, like most of the inhabitants of Burma, are of Mongoloid appearance. They suggested a mix of Chinese and American Indian features, small and physically strong. I felt more like an anthropologist than an ethnologist, however, in my military guise.

During a spell of about three weeks when we were pretty safe and some distance from any Japanese forces, I walked entirely alone carrying a pack and Sten gun, with a little ammunition. But, as we moved forward, the G1 decided that I should always be accompanied by an armed escort of four Africans with rifles, together with an Anglo-Burmese sergeant to act as an interpreter. I do not recall his name, but he became a good friend. His father had been a Scottish police officer in Rangoon and his mother a Burmese woman. He belonged to a small group called the Anglo-Burmese Intelligence Corps, which was very helpful in providing interpreters who were very knowledgeable about the country. With his aid, I was able to question village heads about the movements of the Japanese. Whether or not I was always told the truth I shall never know. However, when simple, only partially literate people are obviously friendly, it is unlikely that they are in fact hostile, and I never encountered the slightest hostility in the hills.

There were strong practical reasons for believing that the Kumis and other hill tribes welcomed our presence among them and greatly resented that of the Japanese.

The cultivation of rice is their basic activity. Elsewhere, whether in India or Burma, most rice is grown in paddy fields on very flat land. The land is divided up into small areas separated by handmade earth walls called *bund*s. This ensures that each little field will contain rainwater of uniform depth of a few inches, the stems of rice plants being planted in rows in the watered soil below.

In the hills a very different procedure is followed. The hillsides are covered with bamboo. Seen from a distance the landscape early in the dry season consists of irregular rectangles or fields of bamboo, some much older than others. Some are dried yellow by the sun; others will be light or dark green and older, some will be covered by big bamboo twenty feet or more in height and several inches in girth. A few of the smaller, corn-like crops will be on fire, with black smoke billowing to the sky and flames leaping outwards.

A brief explanation goes thus. When a patch of bamboo is about seven years old the people cut it down. As soon as it has become fully dry they set fire to it. On the arrival of the first monsoon rain they use narrow metal hoes to mix the ash into the wet, clayey soil, in which they plant rice seed, taking great care to avoid damage to the old bamboo roots. The function of the roots of bamboo is to hold the frail soil of the hillsides and prevent it washing away. The rivers and streams of the country have eroded the landscape into its present form over hundreds of years.

Since the soil of the hillsides has to support both bamboo and rice, it becomes exhausted after a single crop of rice. There are no roads and no wheeled vehicles. So, when all the rice land within walking distance of a hamlet is exhausted, the people migrate to another hamlet site. They select an old abandoned site adjoining enough land ready for fresh culti-vation. There they build new houses with split bamboo, and are often able to use the old solid stilts as foundations. Walking along a stream bank one can often identify an old site by a few poles fixed in the ground and fruit trees (mango or a local form of cherry) growing nearby.

I wondered how a migrating group would subsist for a

whole season of building and cultivation before any fresh rice crop could be available for consumption. They do so by borrowing a stock of rice from a neighbouring hamlet whose people have produced more rice than they expect to require for food and seed. Failure of the crop after insufficient rain or too much of it can mean famine ahead. Every now and then I would see the people of a hamlet on migration. They would tramp along carrying big baskets of rice, together with goats, pigs and poultry all slung on poles supported on men's shoulders. The women and children carried pots, pans and various tools, usually on their heads. In short, a primitive form of productive credit could be seen in operation. A rate of interest would be hidden from view in all this, like the smile of a Cheshire cat.

Another question was: since the hill people had no metal or textile industries, how did they obtain their tools, cotton garments, matches, kerosene, tea and the occasional book about the Buddha or possibly Krishna? All such things were bought from Indian or Burmese traders. During the Japanese occupation, however, all such trade had ceased. The people were in rags. Before the war, the hill people sold some of their rice and a good deal of tobacco, poultry, melons and other garden products to visiting traders from both sides of the border, using the proceeds to pay for imports. To repay a loan, a migrating group would have to produce enough rice both to repay the loan (plus interest) and meet their need for seed for the next year's crop. Rural debt, all over India and Southeast Asia has always been a grave administrative and legal problem.

The reader may wonder why I have dwelt on all this. The reason is not merely that as a former student at the LSE I found it of interest, but that it became for us a factor of military importance. The Japanese, when they reached the hills, had nothing of value to offer to the hillmen. If they used money to pay for rice or anything else, including labour, there were no shops in which the money could be spent. The Japanese had no choice but to conscript the people as forced labourers. The main job of these slaves was to carry on their heads and backs virtually all the military loads and food of the Japanese infantry. In short, they lived 'off the country', as Napoleon's army was obliged to do in the terrible advance to Moscow of 1812. These are the main considerations that explain the hill tribes' resentment of the invasion of their world by the Japanese who themselves must have become pretty demoralized in this remote part of the world, far from their own wonderful country.

On our side we were not only shopkeepers and shop assistants, but also much better situated logistically. South East Asia Command, in its wisdom, set up an organization called Civil Affairs, which established well-run shops at various centres in the hills, supplied by airdrops. In those shops the hill people were able to buy all the tools and other goods they required. Everything came from the nearby industrial base of India, itself under our control. The hill-men, skilled in the use of bamboo, made for us a large number of hutments (known as *basha*s), which provided housing for a field hospital for sick and wounded men, and shelter for troops during the rains. We paid for such services in rupee notes to which the hillmen, of course, were fully accustomed.

Also, they built for us large rafts made of bundles of bamboo and powered by outboard motors. These were used to transport our heavy loads down the Kaladan River. I travelled for several days on one of those rafts and narrowly escaped being hit when we were shot at from one of the banks. The river was deep and fast flowing. The trouble was that it got wider and wider as it approached the sea. It was inadvisable to find oneself on the Japanese side of the river

85

in a canoe as dusk was falling. That happened to me, but, silent among the reeds, I was not noticed. I crossed the river to our side (about half a mile) enveloped in dense white morning mist.

For any army in such a territory, the central problem was that of transport. This was dealt with by a series of experiments. First, between our base at Chiringa and Daletme on the Kaladan River, virtually all the infantry of the division were spread out in single file. All were provided with such tools as shovels, axes and pickaxes. With those tools the troops built a long road into the hills, zigzagging up and down all of them. Our sappers blasted out rock from the hills and made the road broad enough to take Jeeps moving in both directions. This constructional job took several weeks. When the road was ready most of the troops and their loads were transported to Daletme in a large number of Jeeps. I remember the sound of them as they whizzed and zoomed through the hills all day long.

From Daletme onwards, the nature of the terrain was very different. The jungle was often thinner because quite wide tracks led through it, most of them running north and south, but some in other directions towards hamlets and villages. Here the problem was one of thick mud, many Jeeps becoming hopelessly stuck. Not all the tracks were muddy, however. To deal with the situation many (perhaps fifty) white and brown humped bullocks from the Punjab, were summoned by radio. They arrived by air two at a time, in Dakota aircraft, for which we made a simple runway. I shall not forget the bewildered look of these dignified creatures as they stepped down gingerly into the sunlight, and the wide-eyed fascination of villagers who watched them from their gardens. The bullocks were put under the command of a British captain who had had something to do with cattle in Britain. Each individual bullock was led and fed by an

African from the pastoral regions of northern Nigeria and
the Gold Coast. Their commander came to be known as
Captain Bullock. The animals could carry substantial loads
strapped to their sides. Eventually they caused problems of
congestion, traffic blocks of Jeeps and hold-ups of troops on
the march. We got fed up with them and, no doubt to their
satisfaction, they were all flown back to the Punjab. In the
end it was found that men alone, devoid of machines or
animals, could move about in the jungly country with the
greatest effectiveness. Before the end of our campaign all the
Jeeps were sent back to India over the hills, taking with
them the baggage we could not carry on our own backs or
heads. A strange silence followed their departure, a silence
broken only by the songs of birds, the bark of certain lizards
and, rising from valleys, the strange calls of baboons.

✻ ✻ ✻

I have said little about one of the most interesting phases of
my work: track reconnaissance. I was given small air photographs of the land and stereoscopic green and red lenses,
mounted on a little frame, to assist me. This equipment was
useful, but could not indicate the depth of streams, often an
important consideration. On such journeys I was accompanied by a young staff engineer, Charles Walch, who
would appear with a dozen African sappers, and we would
set off as a party, usually about a couple of miles ahead of a
body of troops.

Invariably, we encountered obstacles. The commonest
would be a large tree that had fallen across the track. If it
were not sawn up and removed, a certain consequence
would ensue. On reaching the tree the whole column would
halt. The leading man would put down his head load

(containing his own belongings). The man behind him would do likewise. He would then lift up the load of the first man and put it down on the other side of the tree. The first man would scramble over the tree, pick up his load and march on. By the time all the men in the column had got over the tree, the intervals between the men would have grown from, say, a couple of metres to about ten. The column would then be stretched over a large area of territory and become virtually uncontrollable.

I would ask Charles how long it would take for him and the sappers to dispose of the tree. He would say: 'About two hours'. I would walk back to the officer in charge of the column, tell him about the obstacle and ask him to halt his column for two hours before carrying on. Soldiers become demoralized when they are orders given without the reasons for them being explained. The officer would then explain to the men the cause of the halt.

Sometimes the obstacle would be caused by the need to cut steps up a hillside, to remove traces of a small landslip, or to use straight branches from trees to make a rough bridge over a stream or gully. Although all this was most interesting, it was very exhausting for myself, because I had to walk further, back and forth, than any other man in the division, except my fellow liaison officer with the fifth brigade. Incidentally, Charles Walch remained a personal friend until his death in England a few years ago. He was deeply fond of classical music and would organize excellent concerts in his locality.

The subject of track reconnaissance reminds me of a small incident that illustrated the friendliness of the Kumi people. In one of the hamlets I decided to ask the headman three questions.

- Which of two or three pathways shown on the map

would be the best for a column of our troops to follow in order to reach a particular destination?

- Would he be so good as to provide us with a guide to accompany us as far as the point X on the map? And, finally,
- Could he provide us with a chicken and a few eggs to make a change from cold corned beef?

The answer was a beneficent 'yes' to all three requests.

As a special gesture, the headman gave orders for three kitchen chairs to be collected from as many houses in the hamlet: one each for himself, myself and my sergeant interpreter to sit on in his garden with its scratching chickens and tethered goats. In addition, he ordered women to prepare tea for our party. The tea was entirely green, devoid of sugar or citrus, and most welcome in the heat of the day.

One of the children of the headman's household was ordered to show us the reading book that had been used in the school in the neighbourhood before schools had evaporated with the arrival of the Japanese. The book, printed in Burmese script (which resembles a system of fish hooks), was full of coloured pictures illustrating childish stories. Now, half a century later, what children's books are to be seen in the Arakan hills? Perhaps some reader may know. My four African riflemen, squatting on the grass, watched intently as they held their weapons across their knees.

* * *

On one occasion, our little group spent a night bivouacking on the shore of a most beautiful, slow moving river flowing between sandbanks in which groups of tobacco plants were growing, the scene completely devoid of human beings. It somewhat resembled a diorama in the reptile house of the London zoo, but no gharials (oriental crocodiles) were visible. We chose a spot largely concealed by tall reeds, and so not likely to be spotted by anyone else in the area. Such concealment was almost invariably necessary. Using our portable spirit stove we had cooked a simple meal of stringy chicken broth and put up our mosquito nets on sticks of bamboo. We made as little noise as possible as we sat chatting in half whispers. Overhead, the stars were brilliant and the sky cloudless.

Having taught myself a little about the stars, I delivered a whispered lecture to the men. I remember identifying the Southern Cross and a few other constellations, and concluded with a prediction: 'If you wake up early in the morning before it is light, you will see that those stars over there will have moved to another position, about over there.'

One of the Africans was incredulous. 'It no be possible,' he said, 'I neber heard anyting like dat before.' 'Well,' I said 'Just see.' By the following morning I had forgotten about the stars. The Africans had not. One of them said to me: 'Masta e quite right. I done see de stars go for dat place as Masta done say. We neber tink of such tings before.'

That story reminds me of another. On one occasion I was sent on a mission at night, accompanied only by an armed African sergeant who carried a hurricane lantern. We were then in flat, wooded and very muddy country on the east bank of the river twenty or thirty miles from Paletwa. Through it, leading in many directions, were various tracks, most of them having been made by parties of men moving to or from temporary encampments. I was ordered to find my way more or less due north to a certain spot on the river bank, to deliver a message to some troops situated there. I no longer remember the message.

It was clear that I must move for some time only in a

northerly direction before deciding at what point I should look for another track leading due west to the river bank. After an hour or so of silent trudging, I glanced up at the stars to check our direction. To my horror, I found that we had been moving due south. Had we continued to do so the message would never have been delivered and we could have walked into a Japanese position. Astronomy should be pursued by anybody who fancies a walking tour in the forests of Southeast Asia.

* * *

In putting together these impressions of our existence in the jungle, I have kept in mind the intention outlined in the preface, to avoid the violence of war as much as possible. The result, however, so lacks basic truth that I now feel obliged to include certain violent episodes, however briefly. If readers do not want to know the score they should look away now.

At one stage within a few months of the start of the monsoon of 1944 (perhaps about the end of March), a large number of us, say about eight thousand men, including all the divisional headquarters' troops, occupied a flat, circular area of land almost surrounded by a loop of a river (the Pi Chaung), with steep muddy banks. It lay about three-quarters of a mile from the foot of a range of hills to the west, which rose high above us. Most of the area was covered with paddy fields, but our own position was forested. At one point close to us, the river was shallow and fordable with a stony bottom.

On our arrival in the area, I was ordered to take twenty or thirty headquarters' troops across the river to clear away as much of the vegetation as possible from the opposite bank, in order to create a 'field of fire' through which any enemy would be obliged to cross to attack us. I spread the men out in a line and ordered them to slash the vegetation with their machetes. Carrying a Bren gun, I climbed into a densely fronded tree from which I could command the scene and give some protection to the men if needed. The enemy, however, turned out to be of local, not Japanese origin, and in the form of several hundred large and ferocious red ants, determined to sting us into unconditional surrender. In this they succeeded, but not until we had completed the task in a state of frantic irritation. Formic acid can be quite debilitating.

At that river site we were attacked by three isolated Japanese mountain guns, all completely invisible. One of the principal features of jungle warfare is the invisibility of the enemy. All we could do was to dig ourselves in. We were soon digging frantically until we had created a system of trenches similar to those of Flanders long ago. The Japanese gunners had the sense to bombard us at regular hours, including mealtimes and the middle of the night. On several occasions, just as we were sitting down to corned beef and biscuits, we would hear the whine of shells overhead. Striking the tree tops and exploding, they showered us with jagged shrapnel. All we could do was to fling ourselves face down on the ground beneath the nearest bamboo table. We remained in that position for about a fortnight, during which numerous men were killed. The padre was very busy with burial services and the doctors could do little with the wounded.

The period was brought to an end by two events. First, while on patrol, a group of troops of the Sierra Leone regiment located one of the enemy guns at the foot of the western escarpment. One of their company commanders, an eccentric, rubicund Englishman who always carried an old-fashioned hunting horn reminiscent of the song about John Peel, led a charge towards the gun, blowing his horn as loudly as he could while scrambling through the rice stubble. By the time they reached their objective, the Japanese officer had fled, leaving the gun and his written instructions from higher authority for our men to collect. It was clear that the Japanese had much under-estimated our numbers and assumed that we were black American troops. Just how true this story is I cannot say, but that is the way with war.

Second, somehow the two remaining Japanese guns were pinpointed high on the flank of the range in positions beyond the reach of our own guns. However, a radio message to India led to the dispatch to us of a long-range gun with ammunition. We built a landing strip for a Dakota plane to deliver it. Within a few hours our gunners silenced the Japanese guns. The gun was flown back to India and we moved on. In the changing moments of danger we can think only of ourselves. In the fragility of memory, we think of more.

✳ ✳ ✳

During our progress down the Kaladan River we came to a village area of extraordinary beauty whose bewildering name I have somehow remembered — Mazzegaung Khamwe. Here the river flowed over a flat area of reddish granite, with small rapids and pools of deep and wonderfully clear water. In all directions rose steep, jungle-clad hillsides with outcrops of rock. At the time, about the end of April or the beginning of May, the air temperature was very high, day and night, and the atmosphere extremely humid. All of us, Africans and Europeans, wallowed in the warm water, swimming whenever the depth of a pool permitted.

A few days before we arrived in this area, some of our units had been attacked by Japanese machine-gun fire from foxholes hidden along the tracks, the gunners having been warned of our approach by officers who surveyed the scene with binoculars at observation posts high in those rocky hills. Such posts were linked by telephone cables with the foxholes below.

It was in such situations that our air superiority was of greatest value. We were able by radio to request that reconnaissance aircraft from India should locate the Japanese posts in the hills and that fighter-bombers should destroy them.

One blazing hot day as we luxuriated in the water we heard the approach of aircraft from the west. In a few seconds the attack took place. Two or three aircraft swooped down suddenly from the overcast sky, their machine guns firing thousands of rounds upon small areas in the hills. They dropped several bombs whose crash echoed all around us and, once again, I felt the ground shaking (was that an illusion?) I cannot speak for my colleagues, but my own feelings were intense — an irresistible sensation of relief — I could feel the ease of breathing freely in my chest and a simultaneous horror at the situation of the Japanese in those outposts far above.

* * *

From a position near Mazzegaung Khamwe I was sent on a solitary mission to one of our units located to the west of us, to deliver a message. I remember nothing of the message but the walk itself remains unforgettable. We were now well down the Kaladan River in estuarial farming land that was almost completely flat, only a few ridges of hills separated us from India. During all the previous weeks we had been surrounded by jungle covered hills, the dominant features high above our heads. Now we could look round into a wide rural scene of paddy fields, tiny villages and solitary trees, some with pink or scarlet flowers. Occasional black buffalo wallowed in muddy water. The walk seemed long and, as dusk descended, I found a spreading tree beneath which to sleep on a mattress of fallen leaves, waking about dawn the following morning.

To reach my destination I had to follow a path through boulders and small trees bordering paddy fields. In this area I was shocked to find myself walking among the remains of about a dozen dead Japanese troops scattered in all directions. They had been gunned down many weeks before by machine-gun fire from our aircraft. The figures looked as though they had been killed instantly while running desperately for cover. I approached one of them and found it to be only a dried skeleton whose empty eyes stared at me. Boots, uniform and cap alone were living.

Switch on again now.

* * *

We never reached the sea at Akyab because of the impending monsoon in the summer of 1944. It was decided that we should leave the Kaladan River, march due west to Maungdaw and thence over the remaining hills to our old base at Chiringa. There we would enlarge the encampment by building more *basha*s and settle down for the monsoon weeks until the next dry season, when we would advance into the hills for another campaign.

By this time the heat was intense and all of us were very tired, suffering with jungle sores and prickly heat and extremely sick of corned beef. I personally felt so exhausted that the prospect of another campaign scared me. I felt that the physical strain would be too much for me, whatever the Japanese might do.

We got back to Chiringa after the long march, bivouacking on the way. The village was situated on elevated land above an immense area of paddy fields stretching away to the horizon. Within a couple of days of the monsoon rain, the whole area was a foot or more under water. All the villages were built of bamboo and situated on little hills, the huts sheltered by trees, including many mangoes. The houses are not built on stilts but directly upon the earth. Houses are not, therefore subject to flooding, unless there is really excessive rain. From Chiringa the people of the plains could be seen wading in water and often shivering with cold. As vegetarians living in austere conditions, they seemed to me perilously frail human beings. It looked as if their only joys could be experienced in the precious first weeks of the dry weather, when lovely flowers and fruit suddenly adorn their land.

At Chiringa I was ordered to build a cambered roadway through the encampment, suitable for trucks, Jeeps and cars. The road was to be made of earth and clay dug from two deep trenches, forming drains on either side. The cambered surface was to be covered by rolls of steel rods and wire, to prevent vehicles from churning up the earth or getting stuck in it. My labour force consisted of about fifty African troops. Other officers were similarly engaged in building *basha*s with split bamboo and solid poles.

The men, I think, enjoyed the road building job. While beating down the earth for the camber with heavy shovels, they sang at their work, banging the earth in unison. I joined them in this. Throughout the African continent tasks are performed in rhythmic, thumping movements.

The scene recalled

One day, when the road job was completed and the rain had begun, I went to see the G1 and told him that I did not feel strong enough to face another campaign in the hills. I showed him my jungle sores, suppurating and disgusting.

'Yes, Richard', he said. 'We must do something about you.' Within a few days I was taken in a Dakota aircraft to Barrackpore, near Calcutta, together with a few American officers who belonged to forces spread out over the road from India to China. At Barrackpore I was given a bed in a tented military hospital and treated for several days with penicillin, which completely cured my sores. I was then flown to New Delhi, transferred to India Command from Southeast Asia and given a completely new job to do.

Before we go to Delhi I want to look back at our life in the Arakan hills and to recall a few more small phases of it.

During our long walk along the sandy river bank from which we had watched the stars, we followed a succession of posts planted in the sand, on which I would see lovely kingfishers, sometimes so motionless as to resemble plastic models. Occasionally, one of them would swoop down over the river, plunge and return to its post with a fish in its beak. Sometimes the track led through half a mile of reeds, depriving vision of all but the sky overhead.

During the few weeks after the monsoon we learnt a useful lesson. All the narrow valleys, with their rocky stream beds, were shrouded at night with thick white mist, very cold. The mist condensed into heavy dew, which fell like rain, drenching our clothing and all our light blankets. We found that if we could climb to the top of a hill, the drenching mist could be completely avoided. There, the ground was dry and remained warm for most of the night. In the early mornings we could stand and gaze over a magnificent landscape. Down below every jungle-covered valley was filled with what resembled dazzling cotton wool, very slow to disperse. Frequently, flights of green parrots would squawk overhead.

During the hottest weeks of April, May and early June, when there were no biting insects, we often lay at night directly on the ground, gazing at the stars through the branches of motionless trees. Then came the songs of birds whose notes are heard only in those weeks. One such song consisted just of two identical notes, repeated several times. One would hear the two notes faintly from afar, and then loudly from a nearby tree.

Another call was that of the famous 'brain fever bird'. This, of course, I cannot reproduce in prose. However, it consists of a series of querulous calls, each rising to a higher note than the previous one, but always stopping unexpectedly. It is the unpredictability of the stop that is associated with fever. Avoid malaria in the hot weather.

Finally, there was the barking lizard. At any hour of the day or night, barking lizards behave as though performing a ceremonial ritual. Starting at the bottom of a tree, a lizard would rush up the trunk through leaves and foliage, making a scuffling sound. When it was about twenty feet above ground it would stop and emit a succession of sounds that closely resembled the voice of a British soldier admonishing a colleague. 'F**k you! F**k you! F**k you!' said the lizard, over and over again. Then it stopped. After a few minutes the whole ritual would begin again.

One of our British sergeants managed somehow to capture a barking lizard. He made a cage for it with a light wooden box and wire, and fed it with insects. He carried the lizard on his head for some miles. The other British NCOs called it the 'f**k you bird'. Bird thou never wert.

My services, fortunately, were not continuously required, so for several days at a stretch I would sometimes be able to rest and enjoy hot food instead of field rations.

The scene recalled

One night there was a freak shower of rain, quite heavy. Fodi Sesay had made for me a comfortable bed of dry bamboo leaves, surmounted by my mosquito net hung upon four sticks planted in the earth. We all, Europeans and Africans, slept thus in relatively safe areas. When the rain fell, Fodi spread a groundsheet over my mosquito net. By the light of a very small kerosene lantern I lay reading a paperback version of Tolstoy's *Anna Karenina*, which I had bought in London after seeing the film with Greta Garbo in the title role. I was, of course, in love with her. In the book that night I read a sentence in which Tolstoy refers to Anna's black hair. What a shock! How *could* Tolstoy have got it wrong?

Occasionally, for practical reasons I found it necessary to spend a couple of days at the sixth brigade headquarters or with one of the outlying battalions. On a few occasions such halts coincided with a battle and a lot of noise. Our casualties, however, were not numerous.

Sometimes I was sent on long missions up or down rivers by canoe. On one occasion, with two armed Africans, the journey was at night. On that occasion my main worry was that neither of the Africans could swim. If we were shot at they were less likely to be hit than drowned. I made them keep very still and did all the paddling myself. Every now and then we would hear rushing water ahead. That meant that we must somehow get out of the canoe and tug it up over rapids till we reached the deep water beyond. On such journeys one could see nothing but blackness ahead, or the vague outlines of branches of trees extending over the stream. I would look up at the night sky, which appeared as an irregular pathway overhead. I was on the lookout for small lights, indicating an encampment of our own troops. There I would get ashore to join them.

On one such mission, I wanted to get back to our own

headquarters and expected to see their lights somewhere on my left side. At last I saw such lights and we dragged the canoe through mud and tied it up to a tree. I was surprised to discover that the lights came from a company of Sikh muleteers who were lying asleep beneath their big mule blankets. Although we could only speak to each other in a few words of English, a Sikh sergeant was most kind. We removed all our wet, muddy clothes and were given Sikh uniforms. I appeared as a Sikh corporal. They gave us mugs of hot sweet tea, after which we slept soundly with them beneath one of their blankets. On the following morning, we walked to our own headquarters a couple of miles away.

Towards the end of our campaign we were faced with a dangerous situation. Back up the river just to the north of Paletwa, on the left, or Japanese side, a field hospital for wounded men had been set up in a group of bamboo *basha*s. In retrospect, I think that such an exposed site was selected because it was within easy walking distance of a landing strip built by our own troops. After dropping supplies for ourselves, a Dakota aircraft would alight on the strip and take up a few wounded men. They would be flown to India and transferred to hospitals for treatment not available in the hills.

Suddenly, divisional headquarters were informed (perhaps by radio from a reconnaissance aircraft) that Japanese forces were approaching the airstrip and the hospital area.

I was sent for at once and ordered to take a canoe with an outboard motor, travel upstream as fast as possible, and tell the doctor in charge of the hospital to bring all his patients downstream on rafts already in the possession of the hospital and to get as near to divisional headquarters as he could manage. It was a panicky business. After delivering my message I was to get back as fast as I could myself.

It took me about three days, resting a little at night under cover of reeds, to get back to the Paletwa area. I was very lucky because nothing went wrong with the outboard motor and nobody fired at me from the left bank. The Japanese were very thin on the ground and we seldom knew where they might be at any moment.

During that mission, the spookiest phase occurred early one morning just as the white mist lifted to enable me to see the reeds on the left bank. There I saw three Indian soldiers standing, watching me in silence. The Japanese had under command a considerable force of Indian troops whom they had captured. These men believed that the British were doomed anyway and that, by joining the Japanese they were supporting the Indian nationalist cause. My problem that morning was: were those three Indians enemies or friends? If enemies they could shoot me at once. I had no means of concealing myself.

With my heart pounding, I turned, went straight across the river and was greeted by the Indians, who turned out to be medical orderlies under our command. How and when we acquired them I do not know.

In this narrative of events that occurred more than half a century ago, I recall some incidents more vividly than others. Quite inexplicably, I have no recollection of the medical officer to whom I reported with the instructions to move downstream. All I remember is a feeling of a job done, and I set off downstream myself with all speed.

That was not the end of it. A few days later a large raft containing wounded men, under the command of a doctor, while moving gently downstream, was attacked by machine-gun fire. The doctor was killed and the raft, out of control, became stuck on a sandbank among the reeds on the right bank. The relatively able-bodied Africans, with the orderlies, managed to get ashore with all or most of the patients. Pushing through the reeds they found themselves in a small

Burmese village, quite isolated from both the Japanese and ourselves.

For many weeks, those wounded men were treated as lost beyond recovery. Later, at a time when our forces were nearer to the village, a British officer volunteered to walk alone to the place and bring back with him as many of the African troops as he could. He brought back about half a dozen men. A few of the wounded could not be moved and another group refused to leave because they had settled down in the village with the womenfolk, and some were pregnant. Today, a visitor to that village might see a new ethnic variety of mankind and meet a few white-haired men and women with a story to tell. Should any reader wish to visit that village, I can describe its location to the nearest hundred yards.

Much earlier in the campaign, before we reached the hill-top called Satpaung above the river at Daletme, an even more dangerous situation had occurred. During the stage when most of the troops were strung out in a long line building the Jeep track, there was an outbreak of cholera among the men. The disease occurred among the unarmed carriers of No. 6 Aux. Group. I do not remember the exact number of men who died, but it was well over a hundred. While the track was under construction the two Aux. Groups marched all the way from our forward base at Chiringa, back and forth throughout the hours of daylight. Cases occurred at odd points of the long line of twenty or thirty miles.

Cholera is a waterborne disease, incurred by drinking infected water, and our men were so thirsty that nothing could prevent them from drinking from any stream along the route. Water was everywhere just after the monsoon. The symptoms are grim. The disease affects the whole alimentary canal. The earliest symptoms are acute abdominal pain accompanied by uncontrollable diarrhoea and incessant vomiting. The average time between the onset of the first pain and death is about eleven hours. It must be one of the most dreadful scourges of mankind. The disease is spread also by swarms of flies attracted by the liquid faeces of victims. Our medical officers were both exhausted by walking up and down the column and dangerously exposed to the disease. I, too, was greatly exposed because I had to go on various missions to troops up and down the line.

We were suddenly rescued by the arrival of enough anti-cholera serum to enable every man to be inoculated. I do not know why we had not been inoculated against cholera before leaving Calcutta, or Chiringa, but I think the serum itself was a very recent discovery. Each officer was required to lead a body of men to the tent of one of the doctors, and to ensure that every man was duly inoculated.

When my group of about fifty men arrived, I watched carefully to see how the job was done. The doctor grasped the upper arm of a man in one hand and, with the other scratched the skin quickly with a small tool, applied a dab of serum and sealed the scratch with what looked like Elastoplast with a couple of strips of adhesive bandage.

Suddenly, the doctor said to me: 'I'm feeling faint. I must rest. You can see how it's done. You carry on.' He sank down into a basket chair in the hot tent. So I inoculated about forty men that afternoon. Nobody questioned my action and none of my patients died of cholera. Indeed, no other cases occurred. If no serum had arrived at all, it would not, I think, have affected the result of the war, but our small part of the Arakan could have been lost for months, and many Africans would never have returned to their homelands far away.

Much later in our campaign, one evening just before dark, when the divisional headquarters were bivouacking among the bamboo on the bank of a river, we were suddenly attacked by a small force of Indian National Army troops, who fired about a couple of hundred rifle shots in our direction. Nobody was hit, but the attack prompted an excited response from our own troops who wasted hundreds of rounds of ammunition by firing vaguely into the darkness on the other side of the river.

Suddenly we heard a tremendous noise, as if a thousand Japanese were crashing through the jungle to overwhelm us. The G1, with great bravery and presence of mind shouted somewhat as follows: 'Come on chaps. Rally behind me. Don't try to shoot in the dark. Use only machetes. We'll deal with the Japs, the bloody INA or anybody else.' Such leadership is irresistible. We gathered behind him ready to fight desperately against any conceivable enemy.

During the following seconds I glanced up at the sky to see tracer bullets flying like fireworks across the plain towards the western hills. Then suddenly the figure of Captain Bullock appeared, completely calm. Addressing the G1 he said: 'False alarm, Sir. It's just the bullocks panicking because of the shindy.' Meanwhile, bullocks continued to charge about in the jungle. It took Captain Bullock some time to get them under control. The firing petered out and we managed to get a little rest. Next morning there was no trace of the INA on the opposite bank. We marched all day across the paddy fields to the foot of the hills.

During my solitary phase not long after our arrival at Paletwa, I was sent on a mission, which, I estimated, could be completed in one day before sundown. It involved walking about fifteen miles altogether, much of it on tracks with which I was familiar. I underestimated the time required for the mission and did not get back to within about three miles of our headquarters until dusk was falling rapidly, at about 5.45 p.m.

Suddenly, I heard an extraordinary mixture of sounds:

104

what seemed like a rushing wind together with loud, toothy chattering. I was convinced that a force of Japanese was rushing through the bamboo. At once I flung myself down into a *nullah* (gully) about a couple of feet below the ground and pulled a bamboo frond over myself. With any luck the Japanese would rush past without seeing me. While lying there extremely frightened, I glanced upward. Surrounding me were monkeys, large and small, all chattering at once. I had somehow disturbed a colony of them. Who was most scared, they or myself?

As soon as the monkeys had melted away into the jungle, I got up and continued my walk. It seemed better to disturb monkeys than perhaps a leopard or an elephant. The first indication of our headquarters was the black face and white teeth of one of our sentries, his body concealed by trees. He whispered: 'Advance, Sir, and be recognized.'

10

Chairborne in Delhi

While memories of life in New Delhi between the summer of 1944 and mid-December of the following year are unforgettable, I have no recollections at all of such details as the landing of our Dakota aircraft at the airport and how I was immediately provided with a small breeze block hutment in which to live. Such hutments, in long rows, situated about a mile and a half from the great complex of central government buildings, including the Ministry of Defence, formed the living quarters of hundreds of officers, Indian and British, throughout the war years. In 1980, when I returned for a long visit to India, I found those hutments still in existence and full of young Indian officers, including one who occupied the hut that had been my home for a long time.

I had been instructed to report to Brigadier Desmond Young, director of public relations at general headquarters of India Command and I remember a stout, rubicund, genial man sitting behind a big desk in an air-conditioned office with maps on the walls and piles of newspaper cuttings and press photographs scattered about. He was immediately affable and, to me, most kind. Not exactly a military figure, he had spent his life in journalism both in Britain and India, and, I think, he knew personally most of the editors of the Indian press.

Before saying anything about the job he had in mind for me, he opened a slim file that evidently contained some kind of record of my own life before the war. He was aware of the two books of mine that had been published and of my book reviewing for various journals, including especially the *Times Literary Supplement*. After brief references to such details, he added: 'And now you've come straight from the Arakan.' His familiarity with my past was as surprising as his readiness to mention it.

He then described briefly the nature of my new job. I was to be one of four assistant military press censors, each of us a captain, and responsible to a major, the Military Press Censor (India). People think of censorship as a power to suppress opinions hostile to some authoritative regime. The kind of censorship with which I was to be concerned was not of that kind, but of a purely military nature. It was essential, however. The principal reason for it was that most of the reports written by journalists in India for publication in the outside world, were sent by Indian Post Office Radio and could be picked up by the Japanese, Germans, Italians and any other enemies. Censorship was needed especially to prevent enemies from collecting information about the movements of Indo-British forces in the various theatres of war, the movements of particular equipment and, of course, our own campaign plans.

To facilitate the effectiveness of such censorship, all outward press messages could be dispatched only from the main post offices in Delhi, Bombay and Calcutta. No such message could be transmitted from any post office in India unless it bore a rubber stamp marked 'Passed Military Press Censor'. So much for 'outward' messages. As for 'inward' messages intended for publication in the Indian press, there was no pre-censorship and editors were theoretically responsible for anything they published. However, if it was considered by the authorities that this or that report was likely to inflame hostile anti-British or other dangerous movements prejudicial to the success of the Indo-British forces, those responsible could be prosecuted in the courts and punished in various ways. To avoid such prosecutions, the government established a group of civilian 'press advisers'. Any editor who contemplated publishing an inward message about which he was doubtful, could consult a press adviser. If the latter decided that the message was harmless, the editor could publish it without fear of prosecution. If he thought the message was dangerous, he would inform the editor accordingly. The decision whether or not to publish rested with the editor.

As for press reports originating in India and intended for the local press, while neither censors nor press advisers would be likely to be aware of them, editors would still be liable to prosecution in the same way. All this seemed pretty complicated and I could only pretend to grasp Desmond Young's account of it. I soon picked it up on the job itself.

Then, he said: 'Before you start work you had better have a spell of leave at a hill station.' Delighted, I saluted and departed. The obvious place to go was Simla. Within two or three days I set off. I do not remember the length of my leave, but it was probably about three weeks. I managed to find a chalet all to myself at a hotel in the village of Mashobra, situated at a slightly higher altitude than Simla, adjoining a quiet roadway cut into the side of a hill and leading beneath pine trees towards the Himalayan range. While I hardly spoke to another soul throughout my leave, those weeks enabled me to read, think and attempt to write about the subcontinent to which I now felt I belonged.

* * *

Before I continue I want to record something of the change of scene that had suddenly transformed my environment from that of the Arakan hills to this world of New Delhi as I found it in the very hot weather of early June 1944.

First, sartorial impressions. Dressed in dark green denims, with my floppy broad-rimmed hat and carrying a very scruffy kitbag, I was and felt out of place. Delhi was full of troops of many kinds with a great number of officers, all smartly attired in the decorative uniforms of Indian, British and American formations. Everywhere, too, could be seen young women in uniform, and all the military personnel were mingling with the thousands of Indian civilians of all faiths and castes.

The sunlight was everywhere dazzling and life without dark lenses was barely tolerable. Military trucks seemed to constitute most of the motor vehicles to be seen; there were few private cars. Bicycles were everywhere; there were also hundreds of horse-drawn traps known as *tonga*s and hundreds of manually pulled rickshaws. In such an environment, I felt thousands of miles away from the realities of war. The spectacle resembled a brightly illuminated stage setting for a Gilbert and Sullivan opera.

Before going on leave to Simla I threw away my sweat-soaked denims and cowboy hat and purchased the light khaki cotton uniform of a junior staff officer of India Command headquarters. Most wonderful was a richly coloured velvety side cap adorned with a small golden lion. I forget the colours of the cap, but it conferred upon me an unfamiliar glamour, to judge by the frequency with which I was expected to return salutes in the streets.

Today, at the end of our century, a whole generation of adults has come to look upon the epoch of this memoir as that of 'imperialism' and 'colonialism': derogatory expressions supposedly deserved and ever more to be so. The very idea of a hill station is associated with that attitude. I have listened to British people who have visited India only in the agreeable weeks after the end of the monsoon, expressing the view that, since the great mass of the Indian population could never have afforded to spend the hot weather at a hill station, the British imperialists should also have remained in the plains instead of putting their own comfort first. That opinion is held by persons who have not endured the Indian hot weather and are not acquainted with the history of the subcontinent.

Long before the East India Company built the first hill stations, successive dynasties of Indian princely rulers did their best, at vast expense, to shield themselves from the heat of summer and the intense cold of the northern winter winds. Even before the Mogul emperors, Turkish and Tughlac rulers made palaces below ground to protect themselves from all extremes of weather. The great Red Fort in Delhi contains fountains and ever running water intended to cool the burning atmosphere. Such efforts are not merely a matter of luxury. The work of government, throughout human history, is always extremely difficult. Rulers of every kind can seldom preserve the detachment required by authority at times when the atmospheric temperature is many degrees above that of human blood, day and night for many weeks on end. These are eternal considerations that have probably affected every dynasty throughout the tropical world.

* * *

At Mashobra all my early mornings seemed benedictory. I awoke to a gentle knock on my door. A turbaned bearer with scarlet sash and curly moustache brought to my bedside a small tray with a pot of tea and fruit; then pulled aside a curtain to reveal cool sunlight upon the copper trunk of a conifer. Sheets were cool and did not stick. Pillows were soft and completely dry.

Apart from going for walks in the hills, taking a packed lunch and exploring the streets and shops of Simla, a completely British town reminiscent of Tunbridge Wells, I took pains to prepare myself for the Delhi job by getting to know the names and opinions of the principal Indian politicians and political journalists. This I was able to do by studying all the principal English language newspapers, such as the *Statesman*, the *Times of India*, the *Indian Express*, the *Hindu*, *Dawn* and the *Civil and Military Gazette*, and a few others. As for the nationalist cause, so long as the war continued, I was convinced that it must be subordinated to the supreme objective of winning the war.

At that time, the menace no longer seemed to be in the Middle East, but on the upper Burma frontier, at Imphal and Kohima where great battles were still raging. Mandalay lay far ahead. I would be content to see the end of British rule in India, but only after the frontiers were secure and a workable constitution had been provided for by a British parliament in London. Looking back, I doubt if my way of thinking was very popular among nationalist politicians. As for the Mahatma Gandhi, he appeared to me as a sort of holy Indian Gerry Adams (the present leader of Sinn Fein in Northern Ireland) and I had no use for holiness just then.

I remembered how my father, during the old civil disobedience campaigns, had dismissed Gandhi as a wearisome humbug, skilled at avoiding a plain answer to a plain question, never at a loss for elbow room. I sensed that most nationalist politicians inwardly yearned for some kind of violent revolution, which they were temperamentally incapable of achieving. When at that time British troops scrawled upon walls the Indian slogan: 'Quit India!' what they really wanted was to get back to a world of football, fish and chips and women, a world devoid of empty threats, slogans and humbug. They were not afraid of India, but fed up with it.

Although still a left-winger, my attitude was authoritarian and pragmatic, When considering the kinds of problems that must have faced Lord Wavell, the viceroy at that time, I would say to myself: 'If you had to deal with that question, what would you do?' That question was more important than: 'What would be the right policy?' The right policy might never be acceptable to any of the contenders. Most of the problems facing the viceroy concealed an Irish element somewhere. Irish politicians are not paid to solve any problems at all, but to express their opposition to every conceivable policy that might be put to them. Such attitudes are called peace processes. No amount of typewriting would ever really bring together Mr Jinnah and Jawarharlal Nehru or the Mahatma. And what was to be done about the representation of the lowest castes and the Indian princes in any future legislature? In all such problems, it seemed to me that small actions were preferable to large resolutions.

I thought about these things during my walks in the hills about Mashobra. Sometimes I would recline on a ledge and watch little curls of blue smoke rising from the cooking fires of villagers far below, or look at the movements of a tiny beetle near my hand, apparently identical with others to be seen on the South Downs in England. Should a Himalayan beetle be introduced to a specimen from the Downs, it seemed likely that amicable relationships could ensue with greater facility than if human beings, instead of beetles were involved. I did not read Darwin till many years later.

* * *

And so, back to New Delhi. Within a few days I had been introduced to the military press censor and to each of my three colleagues. They included two Englishmen and a Muslim. One of the Englishmen (Alan Bishop) was an artillery officer who had had much experience with anti-aircraft gunnery during the London blitz. Apart from that he had obtained a first-class degree in classics at Oxford, and took the view that nothing worth reading had been printed after the end of the eighteenth century. He became a close personal friend, but the austerity of his opinions was sometimes alarming. I have no idea how he had arrived in India.

The other Englishman (John Coleman) had been a reporter on the *Daily Express* or the *Daily Mail* and had also been a war reporter in the Middle East. He had been shifted to Delhi because of some abdominal disorder that still afflicted him. The Muslim (Farid Jafri) had been a reporter for the Muslim newspaper *Dawn*, and rather worshipped Muhammad Ali Jinnah. He had a beautiful Irish wife whom he had met in Beirut when he had been a correspondent of Reuters. He had had a good deal of experience as a reporter within India. His home was in Karachi.

The military press censor (whose name escapes me) was a pleasant man in his middle thirties. He had a clipped military looking ginger moustache, which effectively disguised his inner identity. He clearly knew his job backwards. Within a few weeks of my arrival he suffered a serious attack of malaria and I went to see him in a hospital near Delhi. He turned out to be a devout Christian Scientist. As such, he had always refused to take the anti-malarial pill and all other drugs and health precautions that were compulsory for all of us. However, he was not charged with any offence under military law but, as soon as he recovered sufficiently to stand on his feet, he was sent back to Britain for the War

Office to deal with somehow. I was then promoted to take his place and another officer, of Anglo-Burmese descent, was appointed to take my place.

So much for the staff of our office in Delhi. We had three captains at an office in Bombay and a Muslim, Major Farooki, who ran our office single-handed in Calcutta. The Bombay and Calcutta offices were linked to us in Delhi by teleprinter. So much for the machinery.

I explained earlier that military censorship was supplemented by a system of 'press advice', which affected only messages intended for the internal press of India. The office of the press advisers was situated a few yards along a passage from the military press censors. There was much coming and going between us. Editors would seek advice on their own initiative, but every now and then the initiative lay with the press adviser. I mention the detail of all this not only because I found it of much interest, but because it was of some historical importance, illustrating a particularly British way of doing things.

Here are two typical situations. One of us, say myself, while reading through a long message from the London correspondent of an Indian daily paper, would come across a couple of sentences suggesting that the British working class was yearning to see the triumph of the Indian National Congress over the small clique of imperialists who dominated the government of India. I would ask myself: what would be the effect of such sentences on the minds of Indian soldiers on leave in India? Would it affect their morale? It was not my job to decide. I would take the message along to the press adviser's office and show it to the adviser on duty. He might say: 'Harmless tosh. Let it go.' Or: 'Let me think about it.' Or: 'Thanks, I'll have a word with the editor.'

Now, suppose that one of the press advisers, while reading a reporter's script that had been referred to him by an editor, came across something like this: 'Now that our forces at Kohima have received a lot more 25-pounder guns, things are looking up.' He would bring the message to the military press censor on duty and say: 'How about that?' The censor might reply: 'The Japs already know about those guns, so there would be no point in stopping the message.' Or: 'Hold the message till I have checked up with Intelligence.' Or he might decide that all reference to the guns must be deleted from the message.

To help us in making decisions we received every few days from Intelligence an up-to-date list of STOPS AND RELEASES. A stop described anything to be treated as secret and not publishable. A release was anything that had previously been a stop but which now might be published. Occasionally, we would worry about whether or not our decisions had been correct or not. I once lay awake all night suspecting that I had omitted to stop something secret. In the morning, I saw that I had indeed made a mistake, but it was overlooked by all concerned.

All three of the press advisers became close friends. They were responsible to a senior civil servant. When I started the job he had been a European with an Austrian name, which I think was Kirschner, but he was succeeded by an Indian officer with other responsibilities as well. I forget his name.

One of the press advisers was an Ulsterman, James Bartley who, before the war, had been a lecturer in English literature at the university in Bombay. He combined a tremendous knowledge of all the plots and characters in the novels of Jane Austen, and a similar mastery of Gibbon's *The History of the Decline and Fall of the Roman Empire*. All this he associated with a love of whiskey and bawdy stories. His wife Elsa, also Irish, had a good job in one of the economic departments of the government of India. They most kindly invited me to meals at their bungalow near the park-like area known as the Lodi tombs in which could be seen many relics of the Mogul epoch.

The oldest of the press advisers was a dark Indian with a Muslim name (now forgotten) and clipped, military looking moustache. He was a retired district magistrate in, I think, the Punjab. Despite his name he was in fact a conventional Anglican who always went to church with his large family on Sundays. Although he had never left India, he was extremely pro-British. I think he imagined Britain as a green land inhabited exclusively by aristocrats on horseback and their ladies with side-saddles and enormous hats. He was quite well off. He and his wife lived a strenuous social life in Delhi, and I was sometimes invited to rather swagger 'cocktails' with dancing and curry balanced in a spare hand. Like his Ulster colleague, he combined whiskey with bawdy verses. One of his recitations in office hours went like this:

> Dear Lady Featherstonehaugh,
> I really can't do any more.
> I'm covered in sweat
> And you haven't come yet,
> And it's nearly a quarter to four!

I remember him with affection. He should have been given an OBE and invited to settle down in Hampstead, just the place for him.

The third press adviser, Fred de Mello, was an Indian Roman Catholic with a large family. Like myself, he was a graduate of LSE, with a degree in Indian economic history. After independence in 1947, he joined the Indian diplomatic service and travelled widely in Australia, East Africa and Hong Kong. He died a few years ago but I now enjoy the friendship of one of his sons, Roy and his family, who live near London. Roy is a distinguished legal adviser to the government of India.

Looking back, it seems to me unfortunate that among the press advisers and the military press censors in Delhi, there was no representative of the dominant Indian community, the Hindus. It is possible that if the brigadier had attempted to find an educated Hindu military press censor or press adviser, he would not have succeeded in doing so. In that epoch all the most influential nationalists were Hindus. Most of the leaders of the minority groups feared that when British authority was withdrawn all power would fall to the Hindus anyway. To secure the support of minority groups, Hindu politicians were obliged to make promises, especially in the form of reserved seats in provincial legislatures. In Delhi, the hub of political power, an educated Hindu would not be expected to serve the British cause in either of the offices I have described. Hindus did valiantly in the armed forces and on the frontiers, but in Delhi the talk was not especially about war at all.

※ ※ ※

My routine of life in Delhi was sharply divided between the first spell of a few weeks and the much longer period when I was in charge. In the first phase I was one of a team of four officers who worked in shifts round the clock; the office never closed. The shifts were so arranged that, after working a night shift from midnight to 0800 hours, each of us enjoyed a respite of a couple of whole days and nights. During the rest of a week the intervals between shifts could be quite short. In such a routine, it was sometimes difficult to get enough sleep, especially during daylight hours.

The journey by bicycle between my breeze block hutmen

and the office at GHQ took about half an hour or a little less. During the summer of 1944, just before the rain, I found the heat extraordinary. At 0800 hours, after a busy night in the air-conditioned office, I would open a heavy door and step out into the open air. The experience felt as though I had opened an oven door to see how the bread was getting on. Heat seemed to hit one in the face.

I would collect my hot old bicycle from a rack and ride down Kingsway (now called the Janpath) to my quarters, unshaven, grubby and hungry for breakfast. I would prop the bicycle against the hutment and go over to the mess, there to sit down with smart looking colleagues who were about to go to various military offices scattered about the government complex. Breakfast seemed good, even including such ingredients as bacon and eggs. The eggs arrived in miniature and the bacon emerged from cans. Tea was better than coffee, which has never been one of the joys of India.

Back at the hutment I would find the atmosphere stifling. I would fling off all my creased clothing. Next, I would collect a can of hot water (all water was hot, coming from tanks on the roof) and pour it over the bed. Then I would soak a towel in water and drape it over a small upright chair and arrange for a whirling electric fan to blow dry air against the towel and thence deflected towards the bed. I lay down on the wet sheet and usually slept profoundly. When I awoke all was dry and hotter than ever. Once my bicycle had a puncture, which I assumed to have been caused by the heat of the tarmac, which bubbled stickily. While I was asleep a servant would remove my soiled clothes, arrange for them to be washed and ironed, and set out fresh clothes for me to don later.

As for meals, I could take *tiffin* (lunch) either at the office canteen or in the mess, and a similar alternative applied to an evening meal. The choice depended upon my movements and the shift system. Although often sleepy, I made good use of what seemed like considerable leisure, I had somehow acquired for a very small sum all eight volumes of Gibbon's *The History of the Decline and Fall of the Roman Empire*. In Delhi I managed to read the first three volumes. I read also a book intended for tourists about the Mogul dynasty. It is hard to think of more appropriate themes for the leisure of a junior official of yet a third empire. Incidentally, anti-colonialists and anti-imperialists could be hard put to discover any phase of human history entirely devoid of colonies and empires. How otherwise has the human species managed to encircle the globe?

Using my bicycle I rode about the Delhi region, visiting such sites as the Kutub Minar, Humayun's tomb and, of course, the great Red Fort in Old Delhi. The land every-where was brown, stony and hard, the roads gritty and potholed. Dotted about could be seen the remains of ancient tombs going back to long forgotten regimes before the dynasty of the Moguls. It seemed to me that virtually all the archaeological relics to be seen in this part of India consisted of the remains of forts, palaces, temples, mosques and tombs. Nothing remained of the peasantry and the nameless millions whose labour had made every relic possible. Occasionally, some small work of art suggested that the people of the past appeared almost identical with those to be seen in the streets of today.

My Ulsterman friend the press adviser advised me to take with me any one of Gibbon's volumes, together with half a bottle of whiskey. I should stand upon the relics of some ancient tomb, drink as much whiskey as possible and then read the glorious prose at the top of my voice. Making sure that no audience would be aware of my antic, I did what I could to comply. I then cycled back to the prospect of dining with the press adviser and his wife and reporting on Gibbon.

Chairborne in Delhi

Much of my reading took place in a delightful little park surrounded by the ancient walls of what was called the Purana Kila (Old Fort). Within the walls was a winding stairway leading to a chamber thought to have contained the library of the Emperor Humayun. He was supposed to have died after falling down the steps, but how true that was I do not know. Many of the Mogul rulers got themselves assassinated somehow. I formed the impression that the marble floors of great Indian palaces had been custom-built for daggers and pools of blood. Anyway, Humayun was a man of books and for me an attractive figure.

I was promoted to the job of military press censor (India Command) early in April 1945. On several occasions both before and after that event, I would go down to Calcutta to relieve Major Farooki when he went on leave, or to assist him when he was under pressure. As for pressure, the climate of Calcutta especially in April, May and June, is one of the worst in the world. While atmospheric temperatures are lower than in Delhi, the air is motionless and extremely humid. Sitting in an office beneath a slowly turning fan, one streams continually with sweat. If one bends one's head over a paper, drops of sweat fall upon it, and a pool of cold sweat forms about one's midriff. One longs to swim. Fortunately, I was able to do that at the Calcutta Swimming Club, together with large numbers of American and British officers.

Although Calcutta was nearer to the war than Delhi, I did not have much censorship to do there. I did, however, have to vet a number of films. Two of them, I recall, depicted African troops whose black skin was ridiculed. This, I thought, was prejudicial to the spirit of unity required by the war effort, so I cut the passages accordingly. Nobody complained.

In Calcutta, I managed somehow to enjoy an active social

life. I would stay either at the Great Eastern Hotel on Chowringhee, the main shopping street in the centre of the city, or at Spence's Hotel. The former was a big building, air-conditioned, with an excellent dining room, which was large enough to contain a palm court orchestra and a considerable dance floor. The building was always crammed with people of all kinds, including many American and British officers and troops. Spence's was a small, dignified little hotel in a quiet street, where the food was good. I seem to remember original paintings on the walls. The manager or proprietor got to know me slightly, and allowed me to use a small penthouse on the roof. In the hot weather I would take the mattress out to the flat roof, watch the stars and listen to Indian music from a nearby street; I read a good deal of Gibbon up there.

One day at Spence's I met a tall Englishman who represented Longman, the publishers, in India, where many of their books were marketed. He invited me to join a few Indian writers for lunch every Tuesday at the hotel. I did so and greatly enjoyed the discussions of contemporary issues, especially the constitutional problems and the outlook for a presumably independent India. These meetings led to introductions to Indian, European and Eurasian women, with whom I would dine and dance at the Great Eastern Hotel.

One of the men I met was a well known Bengali poet who took an interest in me because I had read the whole of Marcel Proust's *A la Recherche du Temps Perdu* in Scott Moncrieff's translation. He invited me to his large apartment, introduced me to other writers and astonished me by being able to read Proust aloud in what seemed to me faultless French.

I have forgotten the names of all the people mentioned in the above paragraphs.

When I joined the army in October 1940, I promised to

write regularly to my wife. I asked her to keep all my letters because they might eventually make the basis of some kind of book. She did so and I subsequently took the vainglorious trouble to type out almost everything in my own letters. In the hope of discovering the names of people I met in Calcutta, I have read through all my letters from that place. Unfortunately, I find that all such names are referred to only by initials, perhaps because, in wartime, I assumed that security was at stake. The bare initials have not jogged my memory. The letters are too voluminous to publish and a mere selection intended for publication would damage the chronology of the story. It is of interest to myself, however, that the letters tell the same story as this narrative, with a great deal of detail spelled out.

Despite proximity to the eastern front, the social world in which I lived in Calcutta now makes me think of a tropical Bloomsbury during the prime of Lady Ottoline Morrell.

* * *

In the hot weather of 1945, I was fortunate in having two short spells of leave, the first after an exhausting period in Calcutta and the second just before the monsoon. On the first occasion I decided to go to Mussoorie and to stay at the Charleville Hotel. I remembered that my father and aunt had greatly enjoyed a few weeks there after the great heat of Patna. In one of his letters he had described a charming adventure when they had taken a packed lunch with half a bottle of wine for a walk in the hills. They had spent a sleepy afternoon on the grassy bank of a mountain brook. I wanted to see if I could rediscover the spot.

The train stops at Dehra Dun. Visitors to Mussoorie (where cars are not permitted) ascend the steep escarpment

of 7000 feet either by bus or by taxi. I went up by taxi, a
thrilling zigzag which made me giddy and seasick. The
Charleville was situated a few miles beyond the village of
Mussoorie, and visitors were (and still are) taken about in
rubber-tyred rickshaws pulled by four men. As at Mashobra
near Simla, I was given an attractive chalet to myself,
designed for the solitary reading of Gibbon.

In the dining room I made friends with an attractive
Englishwoman who had a responsible job in one of the
government departments in New Delhi, and we danced
together frequently at a hotel in Mussoorie. Suddenly, however, she was joined by an RAF officer who had evidently
been a boyfriend for a considerable time. Thenceforth, I
could only smile to them faintly at breakfast and wish I had
joined the RAF a few years earlier.

I certainly found the little brook described by my father,
and even the grassy bank seemed right. How tender is our
ability to share with another human being, after his death, a
world evoked in a single paragraph of his prose.

* * *

When in 1980 I returned to India and paid another visit to
Mussoorie, I found that the Charleville was no longer a
hotel but had been converted into a special training centre
for newly appointed members of the senior public services of
India. Its former rooms and chalets were now lecture rooms,
common rooms and centres for seminars and conferences. I
was fortunate in meeting the deputy director who took me
over the centre and gave me an excellent account of it.

11

The bombs and after

I was in New Delhi in August 1945, when the atomic bombs were dropped on Hiroshima and Nagasaki. No war memoir of that time should omit some reference to those events. The difficulty of writing about them is great. The emotional impact, in my case, was that of shock. Although I did not then give the matter the attention it deserved, I felt that it would have been morally preferable to allow the war to be prolonged than to bring it to an end by means of a monstrous atrocity. Others argued that, if the Germans, Japanese or Italians had been in a position to drop similar bombs on London, they would not have hesitated to do so. That may be true but, had they done so they would have committed a similar atrocity for a strategic end. In all this I am guided less by logic than by a feeling of resignation. Governments should not be advised to do anything plainly unacceptable to them. It is better to bow out. In Delhi it seemed inconceivable that the Japanese would continue any resistance.

Looking back, I am reminded of an experience at the Burmese village of Kyauktaw. After the Japanese had abandoned it, I was lucky to be one of the first men on our side to enter it. I was invited to do so by a young Shan prince, with the rank of captain, who was an interpreter able to write and speak fluently in Japanese, Burmese and English. At divisional headquarters he became very useful in cross-examining a few Japanese prisoners. The Japanese had

125

evidently fled from Kyauktaw in panic after living a very tranquil existence for many months during which any menace from our side must have seemed negligible. The village huts were full of their personal belongings, including many handwritten letters from Japan, and various official looking papers. All this was gathered up by the prince for close study. Most interesting to myself, however, were several beautifully painted sketches of scenes visited by Japanese soldiers from places in Malaya and Rangoon during their long journey from Japan to this remote corner of Burma. Until I saw those paintings I had thought of the Japanese as 'enemies'. But enemies include artists, children and every kind of humanity.

In my office there was a general rush to go on leave and to look forward to demobilization somewhere or somehow. My job fizzled out before the office was abolished in mid-September.

I remember a small incident at that time. For Indian civilians the end of the war at once implied the impending end of British rule. Hitherto, they had been very cynical about this, especially during the first Cripps mission in 1942. They believed that the British would talk about 'dominion status' and even independence but, of course, they did not mean it. But, by the middle of 1945 there was a change of mood. One of the clerks in my office, an educated Hindu, whispered to me. 'Sir, you are not really going to leave us?' Looking him straight in the eyes I said: 'I am afraid that we really shall be leaving, and very soon now. In future you will have to deal with all the problems on your own.'

I arrived by train at Murree, the hill station near Rawalpindi, close to the North-West Frontier, on 31 August 1945. I chose to go there because, despite the monsoon, Murree would probably be relatively dry. Delhi was hot and humid. My skin itched with prickly heat. I stayed at a small hotel, not a chalet this time, and took with me, not Gibbon but Dickens's *Martin Chuzzlewit*.

The social world of Murree was very different from that of Mussoorie or Simla, both of which were cosmopolitan and heterogeneous. The atmosphere of Murree was military and intensely Indo-British. Taking meals at the hotel were several British officers of the Indian Army (not to be confused with the British Army in India). The troops under their command were Indians of famous regiments, which, for generations had been concentrated in this frontier region when not performing garrison duties in various parts of India. I chatted with some of them in the bar.

All of them could speak the languages of their men and admired them deeply. None had heard about the West Africans far away on the eastern front, and they were interested by what I had to say about pidgin English and West Africa itself. I learnt that, while mastery of Indian languages was obligatory for them, words of command were in English, and English was commonly used for many military purposes. These officers belonged to the Indian world, and would continue to do so whatever the future of the country. If they went to live in Britain they would never again feel any comparable identity of their own. Had I not stayed in Murree (now in Pakistan), almost to the end of September, I should not have become so acutely aware of this.

* * *

On my first evening at the hotel I sat alone for dinner at a table facing a wall a few feet away. Before sitting down I passed a woman at a nearby table who was accompanied by a little girl of about three and a half years of age. As I took my soup I was very much aware of the mother and child behind me. After a few moments of silence I heard the little girl say: 'Mummy, is that man a soldier, a sailor or a Roman Catholic?' She could only have referred to myself. The question was so arresting as to prompt an instinctive response. I turned round and said something like: 'Not a sailor, anyway.'

Our eyes met. Within a few seconds she said: 'Yes, do.' I joined them at her table for the rest of the meal. She was about my own age, perhaps a year older. Apart from the little girl she had two other children, including a son at school in England and another girl of about six, who was in bed with a tummy ache.

After dinner she returned to her chalet to put the little girl to bed with her sister, and then returned to me at the hotel. We strolled over to the club, a single-storeyed wooden building with a thatched roof, from which dance music could be heard. She was a superb dancer, yielding tenderly to the smallest pressure of my hand or arm. The Indian band, stationed in a corner of the room shielded by a couple of palms in big pots, played the tunes of the epoch, including such favourites as *Don't Fence Me In*. The floor was crammed with young officers and beautiful women. As we plunged about ecstatically to the rhythm of *Don't Fence Me In*, the floor shook beneath our feet and the palm fronds shivered. The crowd melted away leaving the floor to the two of us alone.

When we returned to her chalet the two little girls were fast asleep in their bed behind a curtain. Soon we were asleep too, and no owl was heard.

* * *

At Murree I walked alone for miles along tracks in the hills, taking picnic lunches made for me at the hotel. I read much of *Martin Chuzzlewit* and was astonished at the extraordinary descriptions of the American scenes. Could such seemingly impossible characters really have existed?

At other times, especially on rainy afternoons, we played exuberant games with the children, Racing Demon with packs of cards, or Happy Families. At first I was a 'special uncle', but soon became Uncle Richard. I loved them dearly. Eventually, of course, I must return to Delhi. I realized, bitterly, that the enchantment of this life could never be renewed in any imaginary Britain of the future. It could be preserved only in the memories of two persons. What drives me to evoke it in these pages? The answer, maybe, is that I am not the only one. Inscribed on a park bench within a few feet of the spot at which I wrote the above paragraphs are the words, 'To the memory of Rita, *te quiero mucho.*'

* * *

I was aware that my office had been closed down in my absence at Murree, but the Public Relations Directorate, of which I was a member, still existed. I reported to Brigadier Desmond Young who, as ever, was most pleasant. We were all waiting for endings of one kind or another. Indian soldiers who were not regulars awaited instructions about demobilization at their regimental centres. British troops everywhere awaited orders to travel by train to the transit camp at Deolali, there to wait their turns to join troop trains to Bombay and embarkation for England. A strict logical procedure had been worked out for dealing with all such waiting. All moves towards embarkation and demobilization were governed by length of service. I knew that I must wait a few weeks before my turn to move to Deolali would come.

All my former colleagues had already left. The atmosphere resembled that of a once-busy shop in whose windows has appeared the melancholy formula: CLOSING DOWN SALE. EVERYTHING MUST GO.

The directorate was still publishing a few magazines in English, intended for the thousands of British servicemen in India. One of them was called *Victory*, not exactly a high-brow product. I was asked to help with its production by checking contributions and reading proofs. All I remember about the contents of the magazine were two items. First, there was a cartoon depicting a Muslim woman clad in a black *burka*, which obscured her appearance completely, apart from a tiny glimpse of her eyes, still visible through a narrow slit in the material. Such figures could often be seen in the streets. The childish expression 'black bogeys' seems apt. The figure is pursued by a genial British soldier who says optimistically: 'Darling, you have beautiful eyes, I *think*.'

Second, some wit, in an illustrated article, described how, on his return to London, he would start business as a *charwallah* (tea seller) on an underground platform at Waterloo station. Not only would he rapidly make a fortune but, in the process, he would bestow upon the British public a precious cultural endowment from the great subcontinent.

✳ ✳ ✳

On the last evening in September, feeling lonely and disconsolate, I cycled to Old Delhi for a solitary meal at the Imperial Hotel, a fine old building painted in a South Kensingtonish grey, with heavy curtains, standing in its own grounds at a slightly higher altitude above the city. It was, I think, the finest hotel in the Delhi neighbourhood, and perhaps it still is so.

Before going to the dining room I sat with a drink at a table in the well kept garden, watching little stripy squirrels as they darted up trees and along branches to nibble whatever was going. Much smaller than the grey squirrels of Hampstead Heath, their behaviour is similar and equally engaging.

While thus employed I heard a voice just behind me: 'Is that Richard Terrell?' I turned round to see my oldest Indian friend, Ravishankar Bhatt, who had been a fellow student at LSE between 1929 and 1933. I had introduced him to my father in 1931 when the latter had come to London on his first home leave from Bihar.

Ravi had been born in Gujarat about the year 1910 into a Brahmin family of distinction. After getting his degree in sociology and economics he had spent a few years doing financial research for a bank in Bombay. In the mid-1930s he had become chief secretary of the small princely state of Bhavnagar. He was chief secretary of the *Diwan*, or Prime Minister's Council. He was staying at the hotel together with the *Diwan*, Sir Preobashankar Pattani and several other members of the council. They were engaged in negotiations with the financial authorities in New Delhi about the development programme of Bhavnagar state. This included improvements to the docks at the port of Bhavnagar, expanded generation of electrical energy, irrigation projects and education, especially mass literacy. Ravi was too busy to dine with me at once but would do so the following evening.

So, on the following evening we did dine together, and talked for a long time about the constitutional problems facing the country. Although I had forgotten our talk, I see from one of my letters that, when Ravi asked me what I myself thought, I expressed the view that, instead of *promising* independence to Indian politicians, we should *threaten* them with it. We should issue a declaration that,

131

unless they came up with an agreed constitution for the country by a specified date, we should withdraw all British authority, come what may. Only a drastic step of that kind would bang the politicians' heads together. Ravi certainly enjoyed listening to my suggestion, whatever he thought of its merits. The decision actually made by the Attlee government a year later was actually more drastic than my own humble proposal.

During our meal, Ravi told me that he had mentioned his meeting with me to the *Diwan*, who had promptly invited me to join him and the members of the council for breakfast at the hotel the following morning. I rose very early for that purpose. In the dining room, several tables had been put together and the *Diwan* sat at the head of them, a father figure to the others, who were all young men. I remember him as a wiry, middle aged man with a clipped moustache, a white jacket and *dhoti*. Ravi presented me to him and to all the others in turn. Then the *Diwan* said to me: 'Major Terrell, I want you to come to Bhavnagar for a week as the guest of the state.' I thanked him warmly, said I would be delighted to visit Bhavnagar and would seek the permission of my brigadier to do so.

I went straight back to GHQ and saw Desmond Young. Raising his arms above his head he said: 'What a splendid thing! Of course you must go! You can show the flag in one of the best of the states. I know Pattani personally. I'll give you travel warrants immediately.'

I left Delhi on 12 October for a 24-hour journey by single-track narrow gauge railway to the little town of Mahsana, where I spent 12 hours waiting for a connection to take me on by a slow train to Bhavnagar. The long journey on both routes passed through territories then under the administration of Indian princes. Hitherto I had seen nothing of princely India.

The bombs and after

I quote below from a letter written at Mahsana station:

Well, here I am in Mahsana, where I arrived at ten o'clock this morning. It is now three o'clock and quite hot — I suppose about 100 in the shade. I have been for a walk round the sleepy old bazaar, seething with people. There are no other white men for miles and the people look upon me as a curiosity. One pleasant thing I have noticed is that nobody here asks one for *bucksheesh* — the people are far more dignified than in British India. I cannot observe any differences in their living standards. I see a lot of people wearing Congress caps, which means that the movement is quite strong, even here in a state.

The soil all round here is very rich and every inch is cultivated. In the early morning, before the sun is up, the country is strangely like England (I mean England in summer) — all a lush green. I propose to get Ravi or someone else at Bhavnagar to tell me a great deal about the agricultural problems of the state, and I shall make some careful notes.

I am now going to sleep on a bench in this waiting room for a while. I will finish this letter at Ravi's place. I am reading Smollett's letters written on his travels in France and Italy in the mid-eighteenth century. It was not unlike travelling in India today.

For several hours during the first part of the journey from Delhi, I shared a compartment with an impressive looking Indian of middle age who sat in a corner a few feet from me. In the train I had with me two recently published books, Arthur Koestler's *The Yogi and the Commissar* and Friedrich Hayek's *The Road to Serfdom*. The reasoning of the latter, who had been perhaps my most important teacher at LSE, was now fast eroding my left-wing views, which I had held since my long visit to the Soviet Union in 1936.

My companion in the corner noticed the books and addressed me somewhat as follows: 'I see that you have some interesting books, Major.' In that way a long conversation developed between us. His interest was further stimulated when I mentioned my father, whose reputation in Bihar was well known to him. He asked what I thought about India. I do not remember much of my reply, except that I felt that religion seemed to saturate the entire Indian population, including the communists themselves. He could see at once that I was a complete agnostic. 'Yes,' I said. 'I simply cannot believe in any kind of divinity.' He understood my position but went on to speak of a devotional eclecticism embracing all the great religions of the world. I could only express a vague appreciation of such an attitude. Today, half a century later, I am no less agnostic than I was then. The incredibility of any god or gods, whether in the form of a compound, a mixture or a gas, remains. However, at some stage he told me his name, Dr Sarvepelli Radakrishnan. He became vice-president of India under the constitution of 1950, and succeeded Dr Rajendra Prasad as president in 1962. Name dropping to this extent must get by somehow.

I was met by Ravi at Bhavnagar and taken first to his house in the town where I was introduced to his wife and four children. He then took me to the state guesthouse, a new white building on a hillside, looking down on a part of the town. I was the only guest and the building seemed so spotless that I could have been the first as well.

At that time, many of the princely states, including Bhavnagar, had adopted a policy of total prohibition of alcoholic drink. Ravi opened a bedside cupboard to reveal a whole bottle of Scotch whisky, intended for my personal consumption, presumably at night and in bed. It lasted me over a fortnight.

After a rest from the journey and a shower, I walked down to join Ravi and his family for dinner. During my stay most of my meals were taken with the family. All such meals were most graciously served. Each member of the family was given a polished metal dish, deep and capacious, into which he or she would place small quantities of various viands placed on the table by the bearer. In Delhi, the overcrowded conditions of wartime had made traditional graciousness almost impracticable. There, I remembered much standing about in crowded rooms, much talk, beautiful saris and sandals, and grave anxiety about the danger of dropping a plateful of delicious food on the carpet. I never quite managed to balance a plate of food in the left hand, eat with the right and apply my mind to the problem of the Sikhs or the steel industry, all in a single concerto.

I do not remember the chronological sequence of the events of that week, but two or three of them stand out. Most important was the annual state *durbar* to mark the end of the monsoon and the start of a new year. I have already described this in one of my other books.* Here are a few quotations from that description.

The *durbar*, both in the princely states and, on rare occasion in British India, was a ceremonial occasion upon which the ruler appeared before his people and presented symbolic gifts intended to signify his magnanimity and devotion to their well being, and received from them pledges of their loyalty. The great *durbar* of 1903 in Old Delhi on the occasion of the

---

* *The Chief Justice: A Portrait from the Raj* (Michael Russell, 1979) pp. 38–40.

Coronation of the King Emperor, Edward VII, was designed as the grandest *durbar* of all possible *durbar*s, and no doubt was exactly that. The little *durbar* in the small princely state in 1945 (where I was the sole European present) was to me a very special occasion.

I witnessed the ceremony from a solitary vantage point in a gallery somewhere near the ceiling, in an airy white hall hung with glass candelabra. On a platform sat the Maharaja in a splendid gilded chair. Ranged to left and right of him were the ministers of his Government, including my friend the Chief Secretary, and other figures, religious or secular. In the body of the hall, on the floor, sat crossed-legged several groups of people, separated by caste and sex, including Brahmins, the holy caste, prominent *vaisya*s or traders, and the main sub-castes, artisans and peasants, every person dressed in spotless traditional costume. The pastel colourings — turbans, *dhoti*s, saris and other draperies — in that wonderful white hall, made a very graceful scene. Near the platform sat some twenty musicians with their large but faintly tinkling instruments, together with numerous glass bowls of various sizes containing water. By moistening the fingers and gently passing them over the rims of the bowls, clear, reverberating musical chords were produced, which seemed to me subtle and arresting.

As for the symbolic gifts, these took the form of a pile of small parcels of cane sugar, each wrapped in leaves covered with gold leaf, about two cubic inches in size. The pile of presents stood glittering on the table before the Maharaja. At the ceremony he stood to receive the representatives of the people who, one at a time, bowed and held forth their hands to receive from him the little golden gifts.

Next, one morning early in the week, Sir Preobashankar Pattani asked me to join him at his house for a personal chat before the start of an expedition in the Maharaja's special rail coach to a town in the hinterland. He sat on a pouf near the fireplace, the tunic of his white jacket unbuttoned, looking relaxed. I sat in a chair a few feet from him. (The sitting rooms of many houses in India contain fireplaces used only on rare occasions in winter.) The background to our talk was the landslide victory of the Labour Party in the recent general election in Britain. Today, half a century later, it seems strange that, in 1945, many people all over the world were wondering about the 'revolution' in Britain. People compared London with St Petersburg in 1917. Attlee was compared with Kerensky. Would history repeat itself?

Pattani utilized the occasion to compare India with Europe. Europe, he said, was the only continent in the world in which such events as the French Revolution, the revolutions of 1848, the Paris Commune of 1870 and the Russian Revolution of 1917–21 could occur. Such events were inconceivable in India. Nothing comparable had occurred in India for the past thousand years. There had been many changes in Indian history, many reforms and reforming movements, but each of them owed its origins, not to any revolutionary upheavals from below, but to the personal charisma of this or that upper-caste figure.

Why was that? he asked. The explanation lay in the caste structure of all Indian society. Caste was hereditary, endogamous and vocational. And it was sanctioned by religion itself. It was the most powerful social structure in the world. By comparison, the *class* structures of European history, by which Marx was obsessed, were feeble. Their feebleness explained the propensity of European societies to respond to the leadership of revolutionaries. There would never be a revolution in India. Any fundamental change in the caste structure of the country would have to be imposed upon the subcontinent by some external force. Would it come from Russia, from China, or from flying saucers? I listened, thanked him, and did not forget.

Another special experience was the launch of an experiment in adult education in the Gujarati language. This took place in a big marquee, I think in Bhavnagar itself. The scheme, roughly, was as follows. A number of illiterate persons, mostly peasants and most of them women, had been selected by the educational authorities as suitable volunteer pupils. The same number of volunteer teachers from schools all over the state had also been selected. Each teacher had volunteered to dedicate herself or himself exclusively to teaching a single volunteer pupil during a period of six months. Throughout the period the teacher would live in the home of the pupil, joining the family and eating all meals with them. At the end of the period there would be literacy tests for the pupils. The best of them would join another group of volunteer teachers for a further period of six months, at the end of which the same procedures would be repeated. The revolving scheme, extending indefinitely into the future, would not only expand the number of literate people in the state, but also become a source of recruitment for teachers in all the schools of the state.

I was aware that similar schemes were being introduced in other parts of India, and it is hard to believe that they did not achieve some success.

The procedure for launching the scheme seemed significantly meaningful to me after my earlier talk with the *Diwan* at his home. A large wooden platform, standing about four feet above the floor of the marquee, had been erected. Along the edge of it stood about a dozen upright chairs, with a big upright armed chair in the centre. All the teachers and volunteer pupils sat cross-legged on the floor, facing the platform. On the platform, the big chair was reserved for the *Diwan*. On his right sat Ravi Bhatt who was not only chief secretary but minister for education as well. The other seats were for various members of the council. The last seat at the right end of the platform was given to me, my uniform indicating that I had assumed the role of sympathetic observer from the imperial government. Everybody on the platform was adorned with a garland of bright yellow marigold flowers. Everything in India implies the use of garlands at some stage, and the making of them is perhaps the largest industry in the subcontinent apart from agriculture.

I do not remember other details, except that there were long speeches, including one by the *Diwan* himself and, of course, resounding applause.

I have written at length about this experience because it so well exemplifies the views expressed to me earlier by the *Diwan* during our talk at his house. Throughout, the assumption was that a scheme such as this, intended for the betterment of the people, must always be inspired by the natural caste authorities in society.

I wrote my first letter home on 17 October, three days after my arrival at Bhavnagar. I shall quote the whole text because it so clearly evokes the pressure of events upon the limited stamina of one required to respond from hour to hour to the decisions of others.

I have not felt inclined to write since I arrived here on the morning of the 14th. Even now I can only force myself to write something. Ravi has been delightful and my stay has provided a continuous succession of adventures. I can do little more than jot down the things I have done:

1. Visited the waterworks.
2. Driven round the town.
3. Visited the new docks.
4. Been out to sea on a test trip on a tank landing craft being transformed into a ferryboat for the Irrawaddy River in Burma, in the local shipyard.
5. Participated in a Hindu betrothal ceremony.
6. Witnessed the annual procession of the State forces with the Maharaja riding in his motorcar, from a balcony in the town.
7. Been a special guest at the State Durbar, the presentation of the Maharaja to the dignitaries of the State.
8. Visited the town at night and seen some of the theatricals connected with the worship of Kali at the Hindu festivals of Dushera.
9. Driven out 15 miles to a village, visited many peasant homes, asked innumerable questions about the cultivation of millet and other aspects of village economics.
10. Been to lunch as a special guest of the Maharaja at his palace.
11. Met an Indian professor of economics and discussed agriculture at length.
12. Met many local dignitaries at Ravi's house and discussed India till my head spins.
13. Been the guest of the Bhavnagar Rotary Club dinner.
14. Eaten a vast amount of curry at meals with various dignitaries every day — meals taken with the fingers in the proper fashion: many delightful dishes in vast shining brass containers.
15. Been for early morning walks with Ravi and discussed old times at LSE.

The bombs and after

I would have written before, but have been suffering from a severe cold, nasal and gastric. I caught this on the journey by getting my body exposed to a fan while asleep at night. The temperature is considerably hotter than in Delhi at this time of year. Not feeling well I have had to rest every afternoon in order to muster enough energy to carry on with the social round in the evenings.

This evening I am going by train to a special village in the middle of the state, to look at the people dancing at the *dushera puja*, or worship. The festivities are held at night. Tomorrow morning the economist is taking me out to another village to see more of the rural life, and I shall catch my train on to Delhi from another station somewhere on the line. This evening early I am going to have a session with a dear old man who is the principal of the local college, affiliated to Bombay University.

Apart from three ordinance officers, I am the only European here, and I have been treated magnificently.

Ravi's wife is a devout Hindu lady who speaks no English, but smiles at me graciously. There are four children, all very sweet indeed. Jyoti and Priti are two little girls, Mohendra and Nilu two boys. Jyoti, the eldest girl, is 11 years' old and is most pretty. Indeed, I think she is lovely, and I hope she will stay with us in England some time.

I am far too confused in my impressions to write a good letter yet, but many of my experiences have been most important to me, and will influence me much in the future. The most important impression of these people is one of *gracefulness*. The Prime Minister, a remarkable man named Pattani, of whom I have seen a good deal, is extremely charming. He and I have had some interesting discussions about Indian manners and grace. I feel that all the other parts of the Old World are dissolving into a single amorphous Westernism. India will retain her peculiar gracefulness and subtlety — she will remain as a lone vehicle of some of the gracefulness of the whole Old World. The Buddhism of the Far East and the aristocratic tradition of Europe — both survive, in transmuted forms, in India today. The Durbar ceremony, with all the men in their traditional turbans, pink, mauve, white or blue muslins, was like some eighteenth-century European reception. My lunch with the Maharaja was a fantastic scene.

In the above list of experiences there is no mention of the launch of the mass education programme in the marquee. That is because it took place after the letter was written.

After independence (1947), in 1949/50, all the princely states of the subcontinent were abolished, their territories being merged with either India or Pakistan. The former provinces of British India became partly autonomous states within the two federal systems. So far as India was concerned, there was a further change towards the end of the 1950s. The frontiers of several parts of the country were redrawn in such a way as to strengthen the linguistic and cultural homogeneity of the integral states. In 1960, Bhavnagar became part of Gujarat, the dominant language of the peoples and former princely states in the peninsular of Kathiawar being Gujarati.

12
The far horizon

Within a few days of my return to New Delhi I was ordered to go by train to the transit camp at Deolali to await further orders to go to Bombay for embarkation for Britain.

I went, of course, to see Brigadier Desmond Young. He reminded me that, shortly before my visit to Bhavnagar he had given me the job of drafting a speech for him to make to some gathering (I forget what it was). He thanked me for the draft most warmly. And so we parted. At Deolali, hundreds of us lived a makeshift existence under canvas, and I was there for three solid weeks, interrupted only by a few days of leave during which I went down to Bombay and stayed at Green's Hotel on the Marina. I shall now quote at some length from a letter dated 27 November.

SS *Corfu*, Red Sea

I hope this letter, posted from Suez or Port Said, will be a pleasant surprise to you. We hope to be in Southampton on the 8th and perhaps I shall be with you some time on that day.

This is an excellent ship, very fast, with splendid food and service. She is an old P & O boat, was fitted out as an armed merchant raider and served in that role until a year ago when she was completely refitted as a troopship in America.

We were roused from our *charpoys* (beds) at 05.30 on the morning of the 20th at Deolali and left by special train for Bombay, arriving there at midday, at the dockside. You can imagine the feelings with which we saw our grey ship lying at the dock, a sight for which every one of us had pined for so very, very long. I shall not forget those moments, though there was scarcely any demonstration of feelings among us officers. Later, when the ship sailed away, the men stood on the deck with scarcely a word uttered. Remorse at the curses. Perplexity at a mood so unexpected. India, poor wretched land!

On board we found the ship packed with British troops who had arrived before us, most of them members of the famous British 36th Division.

I am sharing a cabin with thirteen others. We are in metal bunks, somewhat too short to enable one to stretch one's legs, but fair enough, for we are moving in the right direction.

I found that the OC troops on board is Lt.-Col. Hayes, DSO, who was my brigadier during our campaign. He went sick and has had to revert to his war substantive rank. I know him fairly well, for I was the liaison officer whose special job it was to liaise with his brigade throughout our campaign. He is one of the few men I have met since I left the Arakan who knew the little *chaungs* and creeks of the Kaladan valley as I knew them. On board I have also found an officer with whom I had shared a cabin on the voyage to West Africa two years and eight months ago. He is now a major and commanded a Gold Coast company until he left the division a month ago.

The planning of life on a troopship is something of a problem. There are about 350 officers and some 2200 men on board. All have to be fed, exercised and amused somehow (though why they cannot simply be left alone for a while is not certain). Hayes has proceeded by creating a floating brigade of these men in a few hours, calling for volunteers among the officers to organize it. There is a scarcity of majors, so I felt I should volunteer to command a troop deck, and this I did. I have six captains and 211 men, and have split them up into platoons, giving each a sergeant.

There are inspections daily, at 10.30 and 22.30, and my lot do PT on the promenade deck from 08.00 to 08.45, in two shifts. At first it all felt like wearisome bullshit, but we have reduced everything to an efficient routine by now, and the moaning has all subsided. I take the PT in the morning and this keeps me fit for a day of reading on the boat deck afterwards. I also take the morning inspections, report little faults in the ventilation system, electric lamps blown, water taps defective etc., and see that the men get their rations of cigarettes and that their grievances receive some attention. I leave the evening inspection to other officers. The whole experience reminds me of my life with troops in England, and I find it refreshing after all the solitary desk work I have done. ... On the long voyage from Lagos to Bombay I was in the galleys cooking for Africans, and enjoyed that, though I exhausted myself unduly with it. Now I find much less difficulty in organizing things smoothly than I did when I last had any troops to deal with.

Later. I have just had a foot inspection and found 11 men with foot rot — leftovers from the Burma campaigns which these men have endured for three years. It is strange how men will leave their physical ills unattended to. I am having them paraded for the

145

doctor tomorrow morning — the sea and the warm
sun are glorious. For five days across the Indian Ocean
the sea was gentle — rippling and blue, with little
white splashes dancing in the sun, and the fine horizon
all about us, taking the eye as far as the line of sight
may go, without any obstruction whatever. On the
deck of a clean ship men abstracted from the con-
tinuum of history may become philosopher-kings,
discussing the affairs of the world at a distance appropriate to the contemplation of value. The sea is a
social world of water by itself. Each wavelet is a life,
with its gestation, birth, career and dissolution into
the endless origin. Like freedom in the world of men,
the freedom of the waves is upon the surface of
necessity. The analogy is endlessly fruitful and infin-
itely pathetic. ... I love all the voyages I have
experienced for the anthropomorphic images that have
occurred to me in the course of them. The sea is empty
of men, yet so rich in its allegorical stagecraft that the
historical simile may be accepted in every generation,
every crisis, every transition.

I am reading solidly through Lewis Mumford's book
The Condition of Man. This I do on the top deck,
sitting in the hot sun. I brought a folding chair on
board with me and am very fortunate to have it. I am
sunburned and well, but have caught a slight cold,
probably while walking round the troop deck. I try to
get rid of it by sniffing up plenty of salt water in the
showers. The latter are another joy on board ship. To
rub the body hard with hot or cold salt water is very
invigorating and probably good for one in some way.

I find that the secret of living during waiting periods,
such as that we had at Deolali, where we had to spend
nearly a whole month with 'nothing to do', or here on

this ship, is to develop a strict regimen of life and adhere to it — certain periods of physical exercise, certain periods of mental concentration and certain periods for some sort of contact with other men (I find the last the most trying). I believe the extraordinary helplessness and lack of resource of most modern men in periods when their doings are not decided for them by the 'managers', is due to the directionless character of our civilization at its present phase of dissolution. Cards, listening to endless jazz gramophone records, reading worthless books, calculating and betting on the results of other people's sporting contests, all are methods of destroying time in which there is 'no work'. Lewis Mumford is very good on the weakness of the utilitarian philosophy upon which the last four generations of Western men have been fed. The supreme end was to produce more and more things, and therefore to consume more and more things. The more the world produced, the more it consumed, the more happiness there would be for the greatest number, the better the civilization. This extraordinary belief was held no less by Marx than by the capitalists of his time, and I must confess that it has been the foundation of my own belief until recently. The history through which we have been living has shaken my utilitarian philosophy very severely. I now feel that regimen, gracefulness, beauty, direction and survival must all be embraced by our philosophy. Direction is provided by Russia, gracefulness by India. The West has nothing but the 'standard of living', a mere frame.

The Red Sea, contrary to what one would expect, is wide — no land visible on either side — and not red at all. In fact it is delightfully blue, with a fresh breeze blowing in the dancing sunlight.

Somewhere in the Bitter Lake just to the south of the Suez Canal we collided with an American cargo ship, which caused some damage to our bows. This delayed us for about three days at Port Said for repairs.

Again, I quote from a letter written on 1 December 1945.

SS *Corfu*, Port Said

We arrived here on the evening of the 29th and found it cold and gusty. The 28th was our last day of tropical sunlight and we made the most of it, sunbathing and reading on the decks. We are now all in battledress or sweaters and feel the cold as a sort of providential imposition. The cold weather seems irritating and stupid. The intense heat of India made one angry and helpless. The gusty idiocy of the weather here is irritating, perhaps because there is nobody or no system to blame for it. The possession of a suitable divinity serves the useful purpose of accepting the curses, as well as the prayers of the faithful. We agnostics and atheists are irritable, for lack of a divine repository for our complaints.

The shore authorities (whether British military or Egyptian civilian or Egyptian military I cannot say) will not allow the troops to see the town, except on an organized route march.

Volunteers among the officers were called for to take them and so I felt the call of duty and offered my services. I duly took 350 men for a dreary conducted march round the docks and railway sidings on the edge of the desert. (I had been told to keep away from the town itself.)

After I had got all the men back on board I went ashore myself and wandered about the town. I bought two boxes of the best Turkish delight and two large slabs of halva — Christmas presents. Having exhausted my reading matter during the last few days I bought a copy of *Hamlet*, annotated by Verity, and a copy of Goldsmith's *The Vicar of Wakefield*, which I am now reading.

(For some reason, in the above letter I omitted to describe how, on my troop deck, I had opened a sort of shop for the men, many of whom wanted to buy Turkish delight, halva or cigars to take home with them. I made a list of their orders, bought all the stuff in the town and had it brought aboard by coolies. Collecting the money from the men was quite a business.) The letter continues:

Another book I have just read is G. M. Young's *Life of Gibbon* which I picked up in Deolali. Also, I have just read Maupassant's *Boule de Suif*...terribly moving. People are cruel.

Our voyage across the Mediterranean from Port Said to Gibraltar was very rough. Most of the troops, including myself, felt too ill for any of the parades, inspections and amusements, and the prospect of a still worse crossing of the Bay of Biscay seemed grim. I remember the misery, and also the occasional swaying glimpse of the rugged coasts of Tunisia and Algeria from the port side.

Then suddenly the scene changed. We emerged from the straits of Gibraltar into clear sunlight, calm shining sea and a display by a large shoal of dolphins, leaping out of the sea in glittering unity, all plunging to vanish again. The ballet like performance was repeated over and over again. 'Look at Us! Look at Us!' the dolphins sang.

And the Bay of Biscay, too, was calm and beautiful. Every

now and then the fin of a porpoise rose and sank discreetly as though shy of human binoculars and troops.

We awoke one morning to the horrible din of our own foghorn and, a few moments later, heard the rumbling sound of the anchor dropping From all the troop decks, only dense white fog, very cold, could be seen. One could not see from one end of the ship to the other. Every few minutes the shuddering din of the foghorn was repeated, silencing all conversation. Men covered their ears with their hands.

Looking straight up into the sky I detected a little blue light, and clambered up to the boat deck. Here I was in dazzling sunlight. Nearby I could see white peaks of chalk rock. And, to the north could be seen the green fields of England, and the brown trees of winter. We had reached the Needles off the west coast of the Isle of Wight.

We spent two whole days and nights anchored there in the fog before it lifted and permitted us to move gently to Southampton water and the dockyard train.

Within seconds of descending the gangplank to the dock I found my wife, standing by an open door of the train to Waterloo. She was very cold, having waited an hour for the troopship to draw alongside.

Passionate reunion, whatever the future, deepens the gulf between lives. The world described in these pages could never become hers. And hers could never extinguish my own.

Postscript

T he personal and minor experiences described in this book ended in December 1945. Today, more than half a century later, they have been overwhelmed, as though submerged, by major events in the history of the sub-continent which occurred in the subsequent few years, including partition, independence, the massacres of hundreds of thousands of Indians, the abolition of all the princely states, and much else.

In this postscript I am motivated by a single intention, which is to contribute a little to a wider recognition and appreciation of Lord Wavell's policies in dealing with the issues faced by the British government in the two years after 1945. The reader may wonder why the writer of a purely personal memoir should today concern himself with such a motive so long after the events. There are several answers. Perhaps the most important one is the domination of my adult life by the personality and ideas of my father, who was Chief Justice of Bihar and Orissa from 1928 to 1938, when he died. His letters, most of them addressed to me, contained an endless stream of comment and prediction about the destiny of India after an assumed independence in a future he never lived to see. It is I who have lived to see it. The experience of writing his biography contributed much to that awareness. A few years ago I edited for publication a collection of letters written from India during the mutiny of

1857–8. And in 1980 I travelled extensively in India and was able to talk freely with many Indians in their homes. This led to the publication of a travelogue. Recently I edited for publication the memoirs of his childhood in India of an old personal friend. In 1973 The Oxford University Press published *Wavell: The Viceroy's Journal*, which, I believe, is by far the most authoritative book about the events of 1946/7. Images of India, therefore, have never been very far from the surface of my life.

Wavell was viceroy during the whole of my military experience in the subcontinent, and my inconspicuous office at General Military Headquarters was situated only a couple of hundred yards from the viceroy's house. I saw and saluted him frequently in the street, and the proximity of such a figure did much to exalt my awareness of his personality and presence for over a year between the hot weather of 1944 and the cold weather of the following year.

✽ ✽ ✽

Lord Wavell's journal has a special importance for everyone, Indian or British, who today seeks enlightenment about events in the subcontinent in the postwar decade. For most people those events are grossly simplified. They are, as it were, first jumbled up and then separated into two human-ized blocks. On one side stands the figure of Sir Winston Churchill, the wartime prime minister, who is supposed to have removed his cigar to declare that he was not disposed to preside over the abolition of the British Empire. On the other stands the Labour leader Clement Attlee, who made history by giving freedom to India in 1947. During my travels in India in 1980 I discussed the end of the Raj with many Indians, whose notions of the past were symbolized by

the stone figure of the Mahatma Gandhi and by crude pictures of Lord Mountbatten and the principal Indian leaders
of long ago. Nobody seemed to have heard of Lord Wavell,
let alone his journal.

Between the end of March and the end of May 1946,
three members of the Cabinet in London arrived in Delhi for
discussions with the viceroy and all the Indian leaders, with
the intention of preparing a constitution for the future of the
country. How was such a constitution to be framed? Who
was to frame it? How was the country to be governed until
the new constitution could be brought into effect? Who was
to preside over the discussions? Where should they be held
and what role should be played by the viceroy himself?

The British ministers were: Lord Pethick-Lawrence,
Secretary of State for India, Mr A. V. (later Viscount)
Alexander, First Lord of the Admiralty and Sir Stafford
Cripps, President of the Board of Trade. In the event, Wavell
found himself in the position of *de facto* chairman of most
of the meetings, some in Simla and some in New Delhi at the
height of the hot weather.

It soon became clear to the British ministers that India
was somewhat more complicated a business than they had
ever assumed it to be, and that the prospects of securing
agreement among the many Indian leaders, was negligible.
Towards the end of May they requested Wavell to let them
have his own appreciation of the position and his advice to
the British government should the talks break down. On 30
May, Wavell produced such a document, which is summar-
ized in Appendix IV of his journal. Its contents are so
succinct, and to my mind convincing, that I wanted to
include the text in this postscript. To do so it seemed that I
would require the permission of the copyright holders. This,
for complex reasons, proved to be time consuming because
of the difficulty of identifying them today. I sought the

advice of Mr D. M. Blake of the India Office Library and Records. He explained that the original document, top secret when printed, belongs to the Crown, together with the copyright. I was, however, at liberty to reproduce it in whole or in part, with a suitable acknowledgement to the Controller of Her Majesty's Stationery Office.

I shall not here attempt to argue the case for Lord Wavell's appreciation and advice to the Cabinet Mission. However, I consider that his advice should have been accepted, perhaps with a few compromises, and that he should not have been dismissed as viceroy. I do not believe that the Attlee government, ignorant of India as it was, knowingly decided to permit the massive genocide which followed its rejection of Wavell's advice. He was demonstrably right in predicting it, however, and it was left to Mountbatten and the Indian leaders, to face the mess that ensued.

Apart from the above considerations, Lord Wavell's journal is a literary masterpiece, a wonderful portrait gallery of the epoch. His achievement as an artist is comparable to that of Goya in the Spain of the Peninsular War.

Memorandum by Field Marshal Viscount Wavell

TOP SECRET   L/P&J/5/337: pp. 373–9   30 May 1946

APPRECIATION OF POSSIBILITIES IN INDIA, MAY 1946

1. The Cabinet Delegation have asked for an appreciation of the situation likely to arise if our present proposals fail, and for a general policy for India in that event. For the reasons given below, it is extremely difficult to predict the course of events, and impossible to have a cut-and-dried scheme to meet all the various situations that may arise.

It must be remembered that India is very nearly the size of Europe, and contains an even greater diversity of peoples and languages, and that there are many different forms of government. The South of India will behave in an entirely different way from the North; the reaction of the States will not be the same as in British India; Bengal has its own peculiarities, and so forth. There are other uncertain or intangible factors, e.g., the attitude of the Indian Army, the staunchness of the Police, the value of the asset of prestige, and so on.

2. The general political situation in the country may be briefly described as follows. The principal party, the Congress, which has long been a purely revolutionary movement,

devoted almost entirely to agitation, suddenly sees power within its grasp, and is not quite able to believe it yet. The leaders are still mistrustful of our intention, and believe that we may take away from them what is offered and start another period of repression if we do not like what they do. They are therefore determined to grasp all the power they can as quickly as possible, and to try to make it impossible for us to take it back. It is as if a starving prisoner was suddenly offered unlimited quantities of food by his gaoler; his instinct is to seize it all at once and to guard against its being taken away again; also to eat as much and as quickly as possible, an action which is bound to have ill effects on his health.

There are many internal stresses in the Congress; and the section which is for constructive work finds difficulty in controlling the section whose ideas still run entirely on agitation and destruction. Over it all broods the influence of Mr Gandhi, a pure political opportunist, and an extremely skilful one, whose guiding principle is to get rid of the hated British influence out of India as soon as possible. Congress will probably hold together as long as it is in opposition but is likely to split up when it comes into power.

The real objective of the Congress, certainly of the Left Wing extremists, is not, at the present, so much to make a constitution, as to obtain control and power at the Centre. Their plan is to delay the formation of a constitution until they have obtained control at the Centre, have succeeded in getting British troops and British influence removed from the country, and have gained [? won] over the Indian Army and the Indian Police forces as their instrument. They then intend to deal with the Muslims and the Princes at their leisure, and to make a constitution that accords with their ideas. They will not swerve from this objective. Whether the moderate element in the Congress can control them, or wishes to, is uncertain.

3. The Muslim League is deeply suspicious of Congress under its present leadership, and more particularly of Mr Gandhi. I think the Muslim League would be prepared to work with the moderate Congress element, if it could get rid of its extreme Left and of Mr Gandhi's influence. The former is only likely to be removed by a violent conflict, the latter only by the normal process of a non-violent old age. So long as the Left-wing of Congress continue to exercise influence, and Mr Gandhi throws his authority unaccountably to one side or the other, it is going to be almost impossible to obtain Muslim-Hindu co-operation.

4. Of the minorities, the Sikhs are the most important from the point of view of this appreciation, since they occupy a key position in the Punjab and can be dangerously violent. They are much divided both in politics and in space; and their reactions are never easily discernible. They are an important element in the Indian Army.

5. The great mass of the Indian people desire to go about their affairs peaceably, few of them have any real feeling against the British, whom they have looked upon as protectors for many years; they do not realize what is happening, or what disorder or misfortunes threaten the country if law and order break down. They are, however, ignorant, and easily and suddenly swayed to violent passion and action; and there is, in every large town and in many country districts, a dangerous element who are accustomed to live and profit by violence and are ready tools in the hands of any agitator. Hatred against the British could soon and easily be roused; and there would then be considerable danger to isolated British officials, planters, etc.

6. The Rulers of States are perplexed and anxious;

they realize that their former protectors, the British, are going, that they will be subject to the agitation of Congress, and that the end of their autocracy and easy living is in sight.

In any conflict or disturbances, the States would in all probability remain generally friendly to the British. Hyderabad, for instance, would welcome the retention of British troops in Secunderabad, and Mysore would certainly be unlikely to raise any objection about their remaining in Bangalore; these two places have important airfields which might be of great value to us.

7. It is impossible to tell how or when trouble is likely to come. It may take the form of very serious communal rioting, owing to the Congress and the Muslim League being quite unable to come to terms. The chief areas would probably be the Punjab, the UP [United Provinces, *now* Uttar Pradesh] and Bengal. Rioting in the Punjab would be likely to take the most severe form, since the peoples of the Punjab are more naturally violent than elsewhere in India. It would also be serious in the UP and Bihar, and these two Provinces, which might be termed the 'Mutiny' Provinces, where the trouble was greatest both in 1857 and 1942, are probably more anti-British than any others, with the CP [Central Provinces, *now* Madhya Pradesh] a good third. Communal rioting in Bengal would take place mainly in the large cities, e.g., Calcutta and Dacca, since in the countryside the two communities are generally separated. Troublesome factors in serious disorders in the UP and Bihar are that the main communications in India from east to west run through these Provinces, also that they cut off Nepal from India.

Or trouble may take the form of a mass movement against British authority, either by Hindus or by Muslims, or by both. This is dealt with in more detail later on.

Almost all one can say for certain is that if serious trouble does come, it will come with great suddenness and unaccountability. I have had some experience of eastern uprisings; in Egypt in 1919; in Palestine in 1937–38; in Iraq in 1941; in India in 1942, and recently in the Calcutta and Bombay riots. All these came suddenly, violently and with little warning. On the other hand, they were all suppressed with comparative ease; curiously enough, the least organized, the smallest and the least violent — the Arab uprising in 1937–38 — was perhaps the most troublesome to deal with. This was probably due, apart from the difficulties of the country, to the fact that it had not been sufficiently firmly handled at the original outbreak a year before.

A widespread mass movement, sponsored by the whole force of the Congress, would be likely soon to take a violent form, even if nominally begun on non-violent lines; and it would probably be beyond our resources to suppress it, at least without very considerable reinforcements of British troops.

8. In all this uncertainty, our best plan is to have certain definite principles on which to act in the varying conditions that may arise. I suggest that these may be as follows:–

(1) Our task is to give India self-government as quickly as possible without disorder and chaos. We must induce them to establish a Constitution for India, get them into the saddle, guide them during the interim period, and help them in every possible way.

(2) So long as we retain responsibility for government in any part of India, we must perform the most essential task of any Government, and maintain law and order with determination by all the means

at our command. In particular, we must protect
British lives and property.

(3) It will not be advisable to risk another conflict
with Congress as a whole; if they sponsor a mass
movement on a wide scale, it will probably be
extremely difficult to repress it; and another
period of repression will lead us nowhere unless
we are prepared to stop in India for the next ten
or twenty years. If there is a really widespread
movement against our rule, we should try and
secure an orderly withdrawal, but not necessarily
from all India, certainly not from all India at once.

(4) We must never, however, allow ourselves to be
placed in the position of helping the Congress to
coerce the Muslim Provinces.

(5) We should remember that there are still plenty of
people in India who are anxious for peace and will
support the Government in its maintenance of law
and order provided it shows itself firm and reso-
lute. We must not allow ourselves to be deterred
from doing the right thing through fear of provok-
ing the extreme elements.

9. The military plan to meet the event of serious trouble
provides for our holding on in the last resort to the principal
ports — Calcutta, Madras, Bombay, Karachi — and to
Delhi. I agree that this is the only sound plan. The scheme
also provides for the collection if necessary of Europeans
from points of danger. It does not of course mean that we
intend to withdraw at once at the first outbreak of trouble,
simply that these are the vital points which we propose to
hold whatever happens.

It may be necessary at a later stage to transfer our troops
from southern India to the north (see paragraph 11).

10. If the above estimate of the situation, general principles and military plan are accepted, it remains to consider their practical application.

If it were the firm policy of His Majesty's Government that, in the event of the main parties failing to agree and either or both launching a movement against the authority of the existing British rule, it should be suppressed, I should be prepared to attempt this, and believe it would have a chance of succeeding, if His Majesty's Government would support me with all forces they could make available and give me a free hand to take all measures necessary to restore order, e.g., the proclamation of martial law and the use of all force at my disposal. It would be essential for His Majesty's Government to make a clear statement of this policy and of its determination to enforce it.

I assume, however, that in the state of public opinion, at home and abroad, His Majesty's Government would not wish to adopt such a policy.

A policy of immediate withdrawal of our authority, influence and power from India, unconditionally, would to my mind be disastrous and even more fatal to the traditions and morale of our people and to our position in the world than a policy of repression. I could not consent to carry out such a policy.

It remains to examine whether any middle course between 'repression' and 'scuttle' can be found, if we are unable to persuade the Indians to agree to a peaceful settlement of their Constitution.

11. We must at all costs avoid becoming embroiled with both Hindu and Muslim at once. Nor do I think that we can possibly accept the position of assisting the Hindus, that is the Congress, to force their will on the Muslims; that would be fatal to our whole position in the Muslim world, and would be an injustice.

The alternative is that, if we are forced into an extreme position, we should hand over the Hindu Provinces, by agreement and as peaceably as possible, to Hindu rule, withdrawing our troops, officials and nationals in an orderly manner; and should at the same time support the Muslim Provinces of India against Hindu domination and assist them to work out their own constitution.

If such were our general policy, we should make it quite clear to the Congress at the appropriate time that this would be our policy and that it would result in the division of India. This might compel them to come to terms with the Muslim League.

12. There are obvious difficulties and dangers in such a policy. It is possible that the Muslims might decline our assistance, though I think it is unlikely; it would mean the division of the Indian Army; and our military position in the NW and NE of India would be weak, as a permanency, as the Commander-in-Chief has pointed out. The actual military operation of withdrawal from Hindustan into Pakistan would be difficult and possibly dangerous.

Further, we should have the large minorities, Hindus and Sikhs, to deal with in the Muslim Provinces; and we should have had to abandon our responsibility to minorities, and our own interests, in Hindustan.

Nevertheless I can see no better policy available; and if it were carried out firmly, I think it would succeed.

13. The position of the States and of Nepal in such a policy must be considered.

The principal southern States, Mysore, Travancore and Cochin, would probably have no difficulty in finding an influential position in southern India. The eastern and central States would have to come to terms with the CP and Orissa.

Kashmir, Baluchistan and the Punjab States would remain within the British sphere of influence in the north-west; and Sikkim, Bhutan, Cooch-Behar, Manipur, etc., in the north-east, assuming that we still retained control in the north-east. There remain to be considered Rajputana, some of the Central Indian States, such as Gwalior; the western States, and Hyderabad.

The rulers of Hyderabad would undoubtedly wish to remain in the British orbit; but with is geographical position and predominantly Hindu population, it would not be possible or appropriate for it to do so. We might remain in Hyderabad temporarily, to assist the Nizam to obtain suitable terms in Hindustan, but we should certainly be there for the shortest possible time. In Rajputana the action taken would depend on the influence the Rulers were able to exert over their subjects. The Rulers would wish to remain in the British orbit, and geographically could do so; but their peoples are mainly Hindu. The same would apply to some of the Central India States, e.g., Gwalior, Bhopal.

The Western India States would probably make terms with Bombay, though some might adhere to British influence, e.g., Cutch.

Nepal would be cut off [from] the British sphere, and would presumably make terms with Hindustan.

It is not suggested that this arrangement should be a permanency; and that we should maintain indefinitely what would amount to a 'Northern Ireland' in India. We should endeavour to bring about a Union of India on the best terms possible; and then withdraw altogether.

14. The formation of an Interim Government is likely to be the crux of the whole problem.

If both the main parties come in, and really try to work the government, all may go well.

I think we may dismiss the contingency of the Muslim League agreeing to participate in the Interim Government, while the Congress declines, since I cannot conceive that a Government formed without Congress agreement could exercise authority in the Hindu Provinces.

The difficult situation will arise if the Congress agrees to take part in an Interim Government while the Muslim League declines. It will be very difficult to refuse to form a Government with Congress members and again to allow Jinnah to hold up all progress. At the same time to give control of all India to a Government in which Muslims refused to take part would be very dangerous. It would be likely to lead to grave disorders in the Punjab and Bengal, and would be injurious to our whole position in the Muslim world. I could probably get a number of non-Congress non-League Muslims to join the Government, but with the League standing out the writ of such a Government would probably not run in the Punjab or Bengal; and there would be serious disorders.

It might be possible to form a Government temporarily, with non-League Muslims taking the seats reserved for the Muslim League, in the hope that this might induce the League to break away from Jinnah's control, or make Jinnah reconsider his refusal.

If this fails, a possible solution might be to allow the Hindus to form a Hindustan Government for all the Congress Provinces; and the League to form one for the Muslim Provinces; while the Centre was a purely official Government, carrying on as a Union Government, until the two Hindustan and Pakistan Governments could agree on terms of Union or Separation.

The dangers of such a solution are obvious, but it might be possible to work out a temporary arrangement on such lines.

15. Even supposing that we succeed in forming a Coalition Interim Government and the Constituent Assembly [is] formed, our troubles will by no means be over. There is also sure to be in an Interim Government controlled by the Congress a continuous attempt to sap British authority in every possible way. A real Coalition Government might avoid this, as the Muslims and other Minorities would not wish British influence to be lessened or removed. It is, however, likely that it will be difficult to hold together either the Interim Government or the Assembly. All we can do then is, I think, to fall back on the policy outlined in paragraphs 11–13.

W.

Index

Index

Bathurst (Gambia), 46
Bay of Biscay, 149
Beggars' Opera, The, 47
Beirut, 114
belly palaver, 53, 55
Belsize Park, 11
Bengal, 65, 75, 155, 158, 164
Bengal, Bay of, 66
Bengali, 122
Berlin, 67
Beveridge, Sir William, 7, 43
Bhatt, Jyoti, 141
Bhatt, Mohendra, 141
Bhatt, Nilu, 141
Bhatt, Priti, 141
Bhatt, Ravishankar, 131, 139
Bhavnagar, 131–4, 138–9, 142–3
Bhavnagar Rotary Club, 140
Bhopal, 163
Bhutan, 163
Biafra, 48
Bihar, 131, 134, 151, 158
Bishop, Alan, 114
Bitter Lake, 148
Black Sea, 60
Blake, D. M., 153
blitzkrieg/blitz, 5–6, 10, 114
Bloomsbury, 123
Bombay, 48, 58–60, 63–5, 70, 108, 115–16, 129, 131, 143–5, 159–60, 163
Bombay University, 141
Boule de Suif, 149
Brahmin, 131, 136
brain fever bird, 98
Bren gun/gunner/carrier, 1, 23, 26, 31, 35–6, 74, 92

Britain, 3, 5, 10, 15, 22, 28, 32, 43, 49, 52, 61, 68, 86, 107, 114, 117, 127, 129, 137, 143
British Army in India, 127
British 36th Division, 144
British Empire, 58, 152
British forces, 5, 27, 30, 33, 35–6, 45–6, 62–3, 57–8, 61, 64, 76, 80, 86, 98, 102, 107–10, 112, 121–2, 127, 129–30, 144, 148, 156. 158–9
British government/rule, 36, 49, 68, 112, 118, 126, 132, 151, 153, 161, 163, 165
British press, 2
Buckingham Palace Road, 23
Buddhism/Buddhist, 67, 142; *see also* Mahayana Buddhism
Bullock, Captain, 87, 104
Burma, 27, 39, 54, 65, 78, 82, 112, 126, 140, 145
Burmese, 82, 84, 89, 112, 115, 125
Burton, Sir Richard, 43–4
Bury St Edmonds, 33
Bushfield barracks, 13, 18, 28

Cabinet, 153–5
Calcutta, 65, 73–4, 97, 103, 108, 115, 121, 123, 158–60
Calcutta Swimming Club, 121
Cameroons, 48
Cape, 48, 57
Cape Town, 58–9
Caribbean, 45
Carnatic, the, 48
Carter, Lieutenant-Colonel, 58
Casey, R. G. (Governor of Bengal), 65

Index

Index

European, 49, 51, 53, 67, 81, 93, 99, 116, 122, 136–7, 141–2, 160

Far East, 28, 45, 61, 142
Farooki, Major, 115, 121
First World War, 5, 45
Flanders, 45, 92
Forestry Commission, 31
France, 10, 45, 59–50, 133
Freetown (Sierra Leone), 46–8
French Revolution, 137

Gambia/Gambians, 46, 72
Gandhi, Mahatma, 112, 153, 156–7
Ganesh, 67
Garbo, Greta, 99
Gay, John, 47
Germany/Germans, 4, 17, 33, 36, 46, 49, 67, 108, 125
Gibbon, Edward, 116, 120, 122, 124, 127
Gibraltar, 149
Godavari River, 66
Gold Coast, 46, 72, 87, 144
Goldsmith, Oliver, 149
Gopis, 67
Goya, Francisco de, 154
Grand Canyon, 67
Grange, The, 41
Great Eastern Hotel, 122
Green's Hotel, 143
Greenland, 48
Gujarat/Gujarati, 131, 138, 142
Gwalior, 163

Hamlet, 149
Hampshire, 21, 29, 41, 43

Hampstead, 11–12, 117; *see also* Hampstead Heath; West Hampstead
Hampstead Heath, 131
Hausa, 52
Hayek, Friedrich, 133
Hayes, Lt.-Col., 144–5
Heath, Captain, 11, 47, 131
Highland line, 46, 57
Highland Princess, 46
Himalayan range, 119, 113
Hindi/Hindu, 66–8, 118, 126, 140–1, 157–8, 161–4
Hindu, 112
Hindustan, 162–4
Hiroshima, 125
History of the Decline and Fall of the Roman Empire, The, 116, 120
Hobart (Tasmania), 70
Hong Kong, 117
Humayun, Emperor, 120–1
Hyderabad, 158, 163

Ibadan, 54–5
Ibsen, Hendrik, 3
Igatpuri, 64
imperial/imperialism/imperialist, 110–11, 115, 120, 139
Imperial Hotel, 130
Imphal, 112
India, 18, 33, 43, 49–60, 63, 67, 63–6, 68–9, 74, 77–8, 82, 84–5, 87, 93–5, 97, 100, 107–22, 124, 127, 130, 132–5, 137–40, 142, 144, 147–8, 151–6, 158–64
India Command, 97, 107, 121
India Office Library and Records, 153–4

170

Index

Indian Army, 127, 155–7, 162
Indian Express, 112
Indian National Army, 104
Indian National Congress, 115,
133, 155–62. 164–5
Indian Ocean, 48, 60, 146
Indian Post Office Radio, 108
Iraq, 159
Irrawaddy River, 140
Islam, 67
Isle of Man, 22, 35, 42
Isle of Wight, 150
Italy/Italian, 4, 36, 108, 125,
133
Izvolsky, Rifleman, 25

Jafri, Farid, 114
jankers, 25
Japan/Japanese, 4, 27, 43, 50,
54, 61, 65, 74, 76, 80, 82,
84–5, 89, 91–6, 100–2,
104–5, 108, 125–6
Jew/Jewish, 25, 67
Jinnah, Muhammad Ali,
113–14, 164
Johnson, Sergeant, 53

Kaladan River, 76, 85–6, 93–5,
144
Kali, 140
Karachi, 114, 160
Kashmir, 163
Kathiawar, 142
Kemp, Jack, 17
Kerensky, Alexander
Fyodorovich, 137
King's Royal Rifle Corps
(KRRC), 13, 15, 31, 42
Kingsway (now called the
Janpath), 119

Kirschner, Chief Press Adviser,
116
Koestler, Arthur, 133
Kohima, 112, 116
Krishna, 67, 84
Kumi people, 82, 88
Kutub Minar, 120
Kyauktaw, 125–6

Labour Party, 137, 152
Lagos, 46, 48, 51, 53, 59, 145
Land Army, 30–2
Lapland, 48
legal aid, 7
Life of Gibbon, 149
Liverpool, 20–1, 45, 49
Lodi tombs, 117
London, 1, 3–4, 6, 10–11, 15,
21, 23, 25–6, 41, 43, 45, 68,
90, 99, 112, 115, 118, 125,
130–1, 137, 153
London School of Economics
(LSE), 1, 84, 117, 131, 134,
140
Longman, 122
Luftwaffe, 10
Lugard, Captain F. D. (later
Lord), 49
Lynn, Vera (later Dame), 18,
25, 60

Madras, 160
Madrassi, 66
Maharaja, 136–7, 140, 142
Mahayana Buddhism, 67
Mahsana, 132–3
Malabar, 48
Malaya, 65, 126
Mandalay, 112
Manipur, 163

Index

Index

Parvati, 67
Patna, 123
Pattani, Sir Prabashankar, 131–2, 137, 141
Peninsular War, 154
Pethick-Lawrence, Lord, 153
Pi Chaung River, 91
Polish, 25
Political and Economic Planning (PEP), 1, 6, 38
Poona, 69–70
Port Erin, 36
Port Said, 143, 148–9
Prasad, Dr Rajendra, 134
Proust, Marcel, 122
Public Relations Directorate, 129
Punjab, 66, 86–7, 117, 157–8, 163–4
Purana Kila (Old Fort), 121

quinine, 81

Radakrishnan, Dr Sarvepelli, 134
Raj, the, 152
Rajputana, 163
Rama, 67
Ramayana, 67
Rangoon, 82, 126
Rawalpindi, 126
Read, Captain Gerry, 73
Red Fort (Delhi), 111, 120
Red Sea, 143, 147
Reuters, 114
Road to Serfdom, The, 133
Roman Catholic, 117, 128
Royal Indian Army Service Corps, 65–6

Royal West African Frontier Force (RWAFF), 49, 50, 52
Russia/Russians, 17, 33, 138, 147; see also Soviet Union
Russian Revolution, 137

Sahara, 49, 51
St Petersburg, 137
San Francisco, 70
Satpaung, 102
Schedule of Reserved Occupations, 6
Scottish, 37, 82
Second World War, 4–6
Secunderabad, 158
Sesay, Fodi, 52, 69, 99
Shan, 125
Shiva, 67
Sierra Leone, 46, 52–3, 56, 60, 71–2, 92
Sikhs, 135, 157, 162
Sikkim, 163
Simla, 109–10, 112, 124, 127, 153
Sita, 67
Sixth Armoured Division, 32
Slave Coast, 48
Smollett, Tobias George, 133
Soho, 26, 41
South Africa, 46, 49
South America, 5
South Downs, 113
South East Asia Command, 85
Southampton, 13, 143, 150
Southeast Asia, 79–80, 84, 91, 97
Southern Cross, 90
Soviet Union, 16, 134; see also Russia/Russians
Spain, 154

173

Index